Current
CONTROVERSIES

Afghanistan

Other Books in the Current Controversies Series

Afghanistan

Debra A. Miller, Book Editor

GREENHAVEN PRESS
A part of Gale, Cengage Learning

GALE
CENGAGE Learning

Detroit • New York • San Francisco • New Haven, Conn • Waterville, Maine • London

Christine Nasso, *Publisher*
Elizabeth Des Chenes, *Managing Editor*

© 2010 Greenhaven Press, a part of Gale, Cengage Learning

Gale and Greenhaven Press are registered trademarks used herein under license.

For more information, contact:
Greenhaven Press
27500 Drake Rd.
Farmington Hills, MI 48331-3535
Or you can visit our Internet site at gale.cengage.com

For product information and technology assistance, contact us at

Gale Customer Support, 1-800-877-4253
For permission to use material from this text or product, submit all requests online at www.cengage.com/permissions

Further permissions questions can be emailed to permissionrequest@cengage.com

Articles in Greenhaven Press anthologies are often edited for length to meet page requirements. In addition, original titles of these works are changed to clearly present the main thesis and to explicitly indicate the author's opinion. Every effort is made to ensure that Greenhaven Press accurately reflects the original intent of the authors. Every effort has been made to trace the owners of copyrighted material.

Cover image by Syed Zargham/Getty Images.

LIBRARY OF CONGRESS CATALOGING-IN-PUBLICATION DATA

Afghanistan / Debra A. Miller, book editor.
    p. cm. -- (Current controversies)
    Includes bibliographical references and index.
    ISBN 978-0-7377-4642-6 (hardcover) -- ISBN 978-0-7377-4643-3 (pbk.)
    1. Afghanistan--History--2001- I. Miller, Debra A.
    DS371.4.A365 2010
    958.1--dc22
                                     2009037783

Printed in the United States of America
2 3 4 5 6   14 13 12 11 10

ED190

Contents

No, the U.S.-Led Military Operations Have Not Benefited Afghanistan

Chapter 2: Can Democracy Work in Afghanistan?

Chapter 3: Should the U.S. Military Effort in Afghanistan Continue?

Foreword

By definition, controversies are "discussions of questions in which opposing opinions clash" (Webster's Twentieth Century Dictionary Unabridged). Few would deny that controversies are a pervasive part of the human condition and exist on virtually every level of human enterprise. Controversies transpire between individuals and among groups, within nations and between nations. Controversies supply the grist necessary for progress by providing challenges and challengers to the status quo. They also create atmospheres where strife and warfare can flourish. A world without controversies would be a peaceful world; but it also would be, by and large, static and prosaic.

The Series' Purpose

The purpose of the Current Controversies series is to explore many of the social, political, and economic controversies dominating the national and international scenes today. Titles selected for inclusion in the series are highly focused and specific. For example, from the larger category of criminal justice, Current Controversies deals with specific topics such as police brutality, gun control, white collar crime, and others. The debates in Current Controversies also are presented in a useful, timeless fashion. Articles and book excerpts included in each title are selected if they contribute valuable, long-range ideas to the overall debate. And wherever possible, current information is enhanced with historical documents and other relevant materials. Thus, while individual titles are current in focus, every effort is made to ensure that they will not become quickly outdated. Books in the Current Controversies series will remain important resources for librarians, teachers, and students for many years.

In addition to keeping the titles focused and specific, great care is taken in the editorial format of each book in the series. Book introductions and chapter prefaces are offered to provide background material for readers. Chapters are organized around several key questions that are answered with diverse opinions representing all points on the political spectrum. Materials in each chapter include opinions in which authors clearly disagree as well as alternative opinions in which authors may agree on a broader issue but disagree on the possible solutions. In this way, the content of each volume in Current Controversies mirrors the mosaic of opinions encountered in society. Readers will quickly realize that there are many viable answers to these complex issues. By questioning each author's conclusions, students and casual readers can begin to develop the critical thinking skills so important to evaluating opinionated material.

Current Controversies is also ideal for controlled research. Each anthology in the series is composed of primary sources taken from a wide gamut of informational categories including periodicals, newspapers, books, U.S. and foreign government documents, and the publications of private and public organizations. Readers will find factual support for reports, debates, and research papers covering all areas of important issues. In addition, an annotated table of contents, an index, a book and periodical bibliography, and a list of organizations to contact are included in each book to expedite further research.

Perhaps more than ever before in history, people are confronted with diverse and contradictory information. During the Persian Gulf War, for example, the public was not only treated to minute-to-minute coverage of the war, it was also inundated with critiques of the coverage and countless analyses of the factors motivating U.S. involvement. Being able to sort through the plethora of opinions accompanying today's major issues, and to draw one's own conclusions, can be a complicated and frustrating struggle. It is the editors' hope that Current Controversies will help readers with this struggle.

Introduction

"[Afghanistan] has a long history of for-eign invasions, as well as repeated civil wars—a history of almost endless war that has created chronic problems of po-litical instability, extreme poverty, and lack of economic development in the country."

Today's war in Afghanistan began on October 7, 2001, when the United States invaded the country as the first step in what would become the U.S. war on terror. The inva-sion of Afghanistan came after U.S. officials concluded that the terrorist group al-Qaeda was responsible for the Septem-ber 11, 2001, terrorist attacks on the United States, and after the government of Afghanistan—controlled by an Islamic fun-damentalist group called the Taliban—refused to expel al-Qaeda leader Osama bin Laden and his group from bases in the country. The U.S. attack targeted terrorist bases as well as Taliban military sites, and both al-Qaeda and the Taliban were quickly expelled from Afghanistan. Since 2001, however, the U.S.-led war has dragged on. Although the war is portrayed as an effort to bring security to Afghanistan, the high-powered bombs and other high-tech weapons used by Western forces also have brought death, homelessness, and other devastation to the Afghan people. But the current war is not the first mili-tary conflict Afghanistan has endured; the nation has a long history of foreign invasions, as well as repeated civil wars—a history of almost endless war that has created chronic prob-lems of political instability, extreme poverty, and lack of eco-nomic development in the country.

Alexander the Great was the first outside power to invade Afghanistan in 328 B.C.E. Later centuries saw several more invasions, and in 642 C.E. Arabs took control and introduced the Islam religion to the entire region. Arab rule eventually gave way to the Persians, and then in 1219 the area fell to a destructive Mongol invasion led by the famous Mongol leader Genghis Khan. After Genghis Khan's death in 1227, a number of tribal chiefs competed for power until 1747, when Ahmad Shah Durrani, a leader of the Pashtun tribe, succeeded in establishing himself as king.

In the nineteenth century, competition between the British Empire and czarist Russia for control of Afghanistan resulted in two British military invasions in 1839 and 1868. Ultimately, the two foreign powers established the boundaries of what is modern Afghanistan and established Amir Abdur Rahman as Afghanistan's king, although the British retained control over the country's foreign affairs. The British finally gave up all control over Afghanistan after yet a third British-Afghan war with the signing of the Treaty of Rawalpindi on August 8, 1919. To this day, Afghans celebrate August 19 as their Independence Day.

Independence, however, did not bring stability to Afghanistan. During the next sixty years, religious and tribal divisions led to a series of power struggles and military coups. For example, King Amanullah, who ruled Afghanistan when the Treaty of Rawalpindi was signed, was forced to abdicate the throne in 1929 after his efforts to modernize the country alienated many tribal and religious leaders. The country's new leader Bacha-i-Saqao, of the Tajik sect, was quickly defeated by Nadir Khan, who was supported by the Pashtun tribe. Four years later, Khan was assassinated by a Kabul student. Thereafter, Khan's son Mohammad Zahir Shah became king and reigned over Afghanistan from 1933 until 1973, when former Prime Minister Sardar Mohammad Daoud seized power in a military coup. Despite Daoud's attempts to bring political, economic, and social reforms to the country, he too was overthrown by a bloody military coup just five years later in 1978.

The 1978 military coup marked the beginning of yet another period of foreign occupation and war for the people of Afghanistan. The new Afghan leader was Nur Muhammad Taraki, Secretary General of the People's Democratic Party of Afghanistan (PDPA), a communist party supported by the Soviet Union. The PDPA imposed brutal, communist-style reforms that almost immediately met with strong opposition from Afghanistan's traditional and religious leaders. Within a few months, the country was engulfed in a violent insurgency against the new government. By October 1979, conditions had deteriorated significantly, prompting the Soviet Union to invade Afghanistan.

But the Soviet invasion only brought more bitter conflict. Soviet-installed leaders were unable to establish effective control of Afghanistan because the Afghan people overwhelmingly opposed communist rule. As time passed, a group of Afghan anti-communist freedom fighters—called the mujahideen—grew into a highly effective fighting force. The United States supported the mujahideen in the 1980s in an effort to destabilize Russia as part of the Cold War rivalry between the two powers. Ultimately, the Soviets were repelled in 1992, when the mujahideen gained control of Kabul, Afghanistan's capital. Altogether, the Soviet-Afghan war cost about 14,500 Soviet and close to a million Afghan lives.

The end of the Soviet occupation only brought more violence, as a civil war ensued between various factions of the mujahideen. An attempt to set up an interim government failed, and heavy fighting among various tribal warlords occurred throughout the country. Thousands of civilians were killed and many others were forced out of their homes. Forces loyal to Tajik leaders gained control of Kabul and much of northern Afghanistan, and local warlords ruled the rest of the country. The chaos of this period soon allowed a fundamentalist Islamic group known as the Taliban to gain strength. In 1994, the Taliban captured the city of Kandahar from a local warlord and thereafter proceeded to impose their rule over most of the rest of the country. Many Taliban were from rural, southern Afghanistan Pashtun tribes, and they imposed an extremely harsh rule that required strict adherence to Islamic laws, sought to destroy all non-Islamic elements of Afghan society, and meted out terrible punishments (including death) to those who opposed their views. The Taliban's treatment of women, children, and minority ethnic groups was especially cruel, and international experts accused the regime of committing massive human rights abuses. The Taliban's downfall ultimately was caused by its decision to give sanctuary to the anti-American terrorist group al-Qaeda.

Following the U.S. removal of the Taliban from Afghanistan in 2001, the United States helped to establish a fledgling democracy in Afghanistan, but the country has continued to spiral toward a new civil war, with warlords fighting each other for power within the new democracy and the Taliban staging a comeback in many parts of the nation. In addition, the economy remains dependent on foreign aid, and crime and corruption permeate Afghan society—including a widespread illicit poppy cultivation industry and a growing opium drug trade. Although Western aid has produced some gains in education, health care, and infrastructure, tens of thousands of Afghan civilians have been killed in the current conflict, and thousands more have been displaced from their homes. Disease, poverty, and malnutrition are rampant. Many commentators have begun to question what the Afghanistan war is accomplishing, other than continued disruption for the Afghan people.

U.S. President Barack Obama sought to expand the U.S. presence in Afghanistan to bring more security to the country, but in the Fall of 2009, the administration began to re-evaluate this strategy. Some observers have called for more troops, but others warn that stabilizing Afghanistan may be an impossible task that diverts the United States from its goal of pursuing terrorists in the region. The authors in *Current Controversies: Afghanistan* address the many challenges facing Afghanistan, and discuss the benefits, risks, likelihood of success, and possible future directions of foreign involvement in the country.

CHAPTER 1

Have the U.S.-Led Military Operations Benefited Afghanistan?

Chapter Preface

After the September 11, 2001, terrorist attacks on the United States, many Americans agreed with President George W. Bush's plan to find and punish al-Qaeda, the terrorist group that claimed responsibility for the carnage, and go after any nations that support or harbor terrorism. The vote in the U.S. Congress to authorize the use of military force in response to the 9/11 attacks was almost unanimous. Consequently, when U.S. military forces on October 7, 2001, invaded Afghanistan—the site of al-Qaeda's terrorist training facilities—most Americans wholeheartedly supported the action. Running al-Qaeda terrorists out of Afghanistan along with the Taliban—the Afghan government that gave sanctuary to al-Qaeda—seemed like a necessary act of self-defense. Afghans also cheered the U.S. efforts; many Afghans had long been oppressed by the Taliban government, which had imposed a rigid, and often violent and brutal, Islamic rule over the country. Much of the rest of the world, too, seemed to support U.S. actions in Afghanistan. Now, however, support for the Afghanistan war may be eroding both in Afghanistan and elsewhere in the face of deteriorating security, widespread government corruption, rising civilian war deaths, limited reconstruction progress, and a resurgence of the Taliban.

Many commentators attribute Afghanistan's downward spiral to U.S. neglect. In fact, Afghanistan has often been called the "forgotten war" because of the lack of U.S. troops and resources directed there. In truth, following the victory over the Taliban, the United States pushed to establish a democratic government in the country but since then has maintained only a limited presence in Afghanistan. Early successes included the adoption of a new constitution and the holding of democratic presidential and legislative elections in 2004 and 2005. Hamid Karzai was selected as the country's president, and a number of local tribal leaders were brought into Karzai's cabinet and elected to the National Assembly, Afghanistan's legislature. In addition, under the agreement brokered by the United Nations (the Bonn Agreement), an international peace-keeping force—called the International Security Assistance Force (ISAF)—was established in Afghanistan to help provide security for the new government. The North Atlantic Treaty Organization (NATO), an alliance of European and North American nations formed after World War II, took command of the ISAF, and countries including the United States, Canada, Britain, and the Netherlands have contributed most of the troops needed for the effort.

Since these early efforts, however, many critics have viewed the international and U.S. effort in Afghanistan as minimal. The United States, critics say, virtually abandoned Afghanistan, instead embarking on a second invasion into Iraq, and focusing the bulk of its political, economic, and military efforts in that country rather than in Afghanistan. Commentators have documented, for example, that the United States sought to minimize the size, geographical scope, and functions of the ISAF. Even today, although U.S. troops make up about 60 percent of the ISAF, this only amounts to about 31,000 U.S. troops, compared with 148,000 U.S. troops in Iraq. U.S. economic aid to Afghanistan also has been sparing; as of mid-2008, U.S. aid stood at only about $11.5 billion compared with $34.5 billion for Iraq. And critics say the reconstruction projects have been badly coordinated and marked by waste and inefficiency.

Meanwhile, support for Afghanistan's democracy appears to be eroding among Afghan citizens due to widespread corruption. Many critics blame the United States for allowing former warlords to become part of the Karzai government. The behavior of these officials, according to some reports, includes rampant bribery, extortion, and violence. Some Afghans believe this corruption is one of the main reasons for the Taliban resurgence, because many people believe even the Taliban would provide more honest government than U.S-supported leaders.

Over time, the U.S./NATO military effort in Afghanistan has slowly expanded. Today there are more than 70,000 NATO troops in the country—ten times as many as there were in 2004. Yet Afghanistan is still not secure, and in recent years, the security situation appears to be getting much worse. Violence in Afghanistan has increased dramatically, and now regularly includes roadside bombs and suicide bombings against U.S. and NATO forces. A draft U.S. National Intelligence Estimate in October 2008 found that the Taliban is renewing its influence in the country, and other sources have estimated that the Taliban may already control 72 percent of Afghanistan, almost everywhere except the capital of Kabul. The heart of the insurgency, however, lies in the southern and western parts of Afghanistan, areas close to the border with Pakistan, where remnants of both al-Qaeda and the Taliban have established their bases. Taliban forces now regularly conduct strikes on U.S. and NATO forces in Afghanistan from these Pakistan sanctuaries. Meanwhile, the use of high-tech U.S. bombs to combat the insurgency frequently results in collateral damage—the deaths and displacement of innocent Afghan civilians.

This changing face of the war in Afghanistan has sparked a renewed debate about Afghanistan and the effects of the U.S.-NATO efforts in the country. The authors of the viewpoints in this chapter discuss whether the U.S.-led military operations in Afghanistan have brought progress to the Afghan people.

NATO's Military Presence in Afghanistan Has Allowed for Improvements

International Security Assistance Force

The International Security Assistance Force is a NATO-led security and development mission in Afghanistan established by the United Nations Security Council on December 20, 2001.

August 2008 mark[ed] the fifth anniversary of NATO's [the North Atlantic Treaty Organization, an alliance of 28 European and North American countries] presence in Afghanistan. Set against the devastating effect of decades of conflict, these five years have witnessed substantial progress in all spheres of Afghan life—from a reasonably stable security situation in most of the country to a massive increase in the number of health clinics and children in schools.

Room for Optimism

Since 2003, NATO-ISAF [International Security Assistance Force, a group of NATO countries contributing to a peace-keeping mission in Afghanistan] has gradually extended its reach and is now responsible for security across the whole country. The number of our troops has grown steadily from the initial 5,000 in Kabul [Afghanistan's capital] to the current 47,000 ISAF personnel in theatre. Today, large parts of the country are relatively stable with no or very few security incidents per month even if the security situation in southern Afghanistan and parts of the East remains challenging for international and Afghan security forces.

There is room for cautious optimism. In 2007, the direct engagement of Afghan National Army (ANA) and ISAF rou-

International Security Assistance Force, *Progress in Afghanistan: Bucharest Summit, April 2–4, 2008*. Brussels, Belgium: International Security Assistance Force, NATO, 2008. Reproduced by permission.

tinely defeated militants. Although the overall number of security incidents across Afghanistan has increased, this corresponds to the expansion of Afghan National Security Forces (ANSF) and NATO-ISAF operations to areas formerly considered to be extremist strongholds. In 2007, 70% of security incidents were confined to 10% of Afghanistan's 398 Districts. These districts contain less than 6% of the Afghan population.

Military success has allowed for significant strides in reconstruction and development in many areas as well as helping support improvements in governance.

This progress would not be possible without the increasing effectiveness of our Afghan partners. The ANA is becoming a professional, well-trained and equipped force that will be able to fully provide for its country's security. In 2002, there was no ANA to speak of. Today, the ANA stands at around 50,000; every two weeks, the Kabul Military Training Centre graduates 1,100 more soldiers. The ANA is increasingly taking the lead in security operations and played a key role in liberating Musa Qala [a town north of Helmand Province] from Taleban [a fundamentalist Islamic militia] extremists in December 2007. Ninety per cent of the Afghan public sees the ANA as an honest and fair institution. The evolution of the ANA and particularly the ANP [Afghanistan National Police] are essential pillars in building an Afghanistan that is at peace with itself and its neighbours.

Progress in Reconstruction and Development

Although the security situation remains challenging, military success has allowed for significant strides in reconstruction and development in many areas as well as helping support improvements in governance at both national and local levels. ISAF's operations are providing the space and opportunities for economic and political progress. In some parts of the country ISAF's routine presence is sufficient to allow construction and development to blossom. Elsewhere, ISAF is fighting for the space to allow reconstruction and development to begin. Musa Qala was an important example.

More than 4,000 km of roads have been built where only 50 km existed in 2001, the rehabilitation of the North-East power system has advanced and access of the rural households to electricity has been significantly increased. In 2007 alone, ISAF nations completed 1,080 civil-military cooperation (CIMIC) projects.

Afghan-led programmes, such as the National Solidarity Programme (NSP), have been increasingly successful. Since its foundation, the NSP has allowed two thirds of Afghan communities (more than 20,000 villages) to finance rural development projects worth up to USD [U.S. dollars] 60,000 each.

In a young nation where the median age is 17.5, 2,000 schools were built or repaired in the last five years and around 6.4 million children (including 1.5 million girls) are now in schools.

Since 2001, both infant and under-five mortality has declined by 26% and 22% respectively.

In 2001, 8% of Afghans had access to some form of healthcare. Now more than 80% of the population has access to medical care.

The influence of the narcotics trade continues to hamper progress in key areas: security, governance, economic development and, increasingly, health.

Despite all this progress, significant challenges remain. These continue to be addressed by NATO-ISAF in concert with our Afghan partners as well as the UN [United Nations] Assistance Mission in Afghanistan (UNAMA) and other key international actors.

ISAF's Provincial Reconstruction Teams (PRTs) have supported their local partners and representatives of the relevant ministries on governance issues, including the reform of the justice system, and routinely take part in local *shuras* [a body that provides counsel to a leader]. They have also been instrumental in developing, with their Afghan partners, all 34 Provincial Development Plans that will help implement the Afghan National Development Strategy (ANDS), the country's main national planning and budgeting exercise and principal poverty reduction strategy.

One of Afghanistan's toughest challenges remains narcotics. Although 80% of Afghans feel that poppy cultivation is wrong, Afghanistan still produces 93% of the world's supply of opium. The influence of the narcotics trade continues to hamper progress in key areas: security, governance, economic development and, increasingly, health. That being said, some encouraging developments have been recorded in recent years due to Afghan-led and international community-supported efforts. These include that the non-opium economy has grown at an average of 12% over the past four years, the number of poppy-free provinces has grown from six in 2006 to 13 in 2007.

Afghan public support for international involvement in Afghanistan remains high with around 70% of Afghans supporting the presence of international forces. The majority of Afghans believe their country is going in the right direction and 84% support their current government (as opposed to 4% who would support the Taleban). They also maintain a positive view of reconstruction efforts with 63% saying that reconstruction efforts in their area have been effective since 2002.

Real Political and Economic Progress Has Been Made in the Past Seven Years

GlobalSecurity.org

GlobalSecurity.org is a provider of background information and developing news stories in the fields of defense, space, intelligence, weapons of mass destruction, and homeland security.

After the attacks of September 11, 2001, the United States and our international partners toppled the Taliban [a fundamentalist Islamic militia] regime in Afghanistan, ending years of brutal misrule and denying al Qaeda [an international terrorist network led by Osama bin Laden] a safe haven from which to launch its attacks. The United States is committed to helping Afghanistan recover from decades of strife, and preventing it from ever again becoming a safe haven for terrorists. Our strategic goals remain that Afghanistan is: 1) a reliable, stable ally in the War on Terror; 2) moderate and democratic, with a thriving private sector economy; 3) capable of governing its territory and borders; and 4) respectful of the rights of all its citizens. Achieving these goals requires the application of a whole-of-government approach, along multiple lines of operation, including security, governance, and development. This [viewpoint] describes both the progress we are making in achieving our national objectives, and the challenges we continue to face.

Security

Although security remains fragile in many parts of Afghanistan, our counterinsurgency approach demonstrates how a combination of military and non-military resources can be integrated to create a stable and secure environment, and to connect the Afghan people with their government. Khowst Province is an example. Khowst [in eastern Afghanistan] was once considered ungovernable and one of the most dangerous provinces in Afghanistan. Today, tangible improvements in security, governance, reconstruction, and development are being made. These improvements are achieved through the closely coordinated efforts of the local government, the Afghanistan National Security Forces (ANSF), international organizations, as well as U.S. military, diplomatic, and development experts. Importantly, lessons learned from the successes in Khowst are being shared with our partners and applied elsewhere in the country.

The increase in U.S. forces in the spring of 2008 reinforced Afghan and international forces' momentum and is enabling accelerated growth of the ANSF. On February 5, 2008 the Joint Coordination and Monitoring Board (JCMB) approved a proposal to expand the authorized end strength of the Afghan National Army (ANA) from 70,000 to 80,000 personnel. The Combined Security Transition Command–Afghanistan (CSTC-A) is scheduled to complete the fielding of 80,000 ANA personnel by the end of 2010. Meanwhile, a U.S. Marine Corps Marine Air Ground Task Force is deploying to bolster NATO [North Atlantic Treaty Organization, an alliance of European and North American countries] International Security Assistance Force (ISAF) maneuver forces in Regional Command–South.

Despite many positive developments, Afghanistan continues to face challenges.

The ANA has taken the lead in more than 30 significant operations to date and has demonstrated increasing competence, effectiveness and professionalism. Operation MAIWAND, executed in the summer of 2007 in the Andar District of Ghazni Province, is just one example of the ANA's progress. Planned, rehearsed, and executed under the direction of the Afghan 203rd Corps Commander, a combined ANA and ISAF task force cleared the entire district and removed a Taliban shadow governor. This well-integrated security operation was quickly exploited with the synchronized application of governance and development efforts consisting of medical treatment for 2,300 citizens, 10 new schools, the delivery of 260 tons of humanitarian aid, and one million dollars committed toward additional development. This operation resulted in the significant disruption to enemy forces in Ghazni Province and is a manifestation of the growth and maturation of ANSF as well as the spread of governance and development.

The Afghanistan National Police (ANP) are improving, although at a slower pace than the ANA. Generally, police development has been hindered by a lack of reform, corruption, insufficient U.S. military trainers and advisors, and a lack of unity of effort within the international community. A new CSTC-A–led Focused District Development (FDD) plan, implemented in late 2007, shows promise. This initiative withdraws the locally based Afghan Uniform Police (AUP) from selected districts, replacing them temporarily with highly trained and effective Afghan National Civil Order Police (ANCOP). The AUP then receive two months of immersion training and equipping in a concentrated program of instruction by carefully selected civilian police mentors, with the goal of increasing their professional capability and their confidence to conduct law enforcement activities. Following their collective training, the AUP return to their districts with enhanced capabilities and better able to serve their communities.

Continuing Security Challenges

Despite many positive developments, Afghanistan continues to face challenges. The Taliban regrouped after its fall from power and have coalesced into a resilient insurgency. It now poses a challenge to the Afghan Government's authority in some rural areas. Insurgent violence increased in 2007, most visibly in the form of asymmetric attacks as Afghan and international forces' relentless pressure forced the insurgents to shift the majority of its effort to targeting police and civilians. More than 6,500 people died as a result of suicide attacks, roadside bombs, and combat-related violence. The 2007 ISAF and ANSF military campaign caused setbacks to the Afghan insurgency, including leadership losses and the loss of some key safe-havens in Afghanistan. Despite these setbacks, the Taliban is likely to maintain or even increase the scope and pace of its terrorist attacks and bombings in 2008. The Taliban will challenge the control of the Afghan government in rural areas, especially in the south and east. The Taliban will also probably attempt to increase its presence in the west and north. Up to the first quarter of 2008, the most significant threat to stability in the north and west of the country has come from warlords, criminals, and drug traffickers. The power of these entities is increasingly challenged by the growing competence of local and national government.

Narcotics remain a significant challenge for Afghanistan and the international community. While progress has been made in some areas, overall counternarcotics efforts in Afghanistan have not been successful. As Secretary of Defense Robert Gates stated in his testimony to the House Armed Service Committee on December 11, 2007, "[T]he drug trade continues to threaten the foundations of Afghan society and [the] young government [of Afghanistan]." Opium production in Afghanistan increased substantially in 2007. The narcotics trade dissuades work and investment in legitimate activities, provides the insurgents with a lucrative source of funding, and contributes heavily to heroin addiction in Central Asia, Europe and increasingly East Africa. Although counternarcotics (CN) efforts have resulted in gains over the past six years, the battle against drug traffickers is ongoing, and will be for some time. In conjunction with the Afghan Ministry of Defense (MOD), CSTC-A is assisting with the development and fielding of a new CN infantry kandak (battalion) for the purpose of providing force protection to poppy eradicators. This unit will shortly be put into action and will provide protection for eradication teams to complete their mandates.

Since 2001, Afghanistan has made significant progress rebuilding its national political institutions.

Governance and Human Rights

Afghanistan was the prime example of a failed state in 2001. Aside from the Taliban's enforcement of its version of sharia law [Islamic religious law], most functions of government were non-existent. There were few social services and little investment in health, education, roads, power, or water. Afghans were denied participation in their government, enjoyed no civil or political liberties, and were afforded no avenue of dissent.

Since 2001, Afghanistan has made significant progress rebuilding its national political institutions. Afghans wrote and passed a new Constitution in 2004; 8.1 million people voted in the nation's first presidential election; and 6.4 million voters helped reestablish their National Assembly after 32 years without a legislature. Ministries are increasingly capable of executing their responsibilities, particularly the ministries of Defense, Foreign Affairs, and Finance. Since 2006, the Supreme Court has been headed by an internationally respected and highly capable jurist with a formal legal education.

The international community continues to help develop Afghanistan's justice sector and provincial governments. Progress is slow, in part because of Afghanistan's human capital shortage. Only three in ten Afghans can read, leaving a very shallow pool of literate citizens to staff the courts, government offices, police, armed forces, or private enterprises.

Despite important progress made since 2001, Afghanistan's human rights record remains poor. Though most human rights violations are perpetrated by the Taliban-led insurgency, weak governmental and traditional institutions, corruption, narcotics trafficking, and the country's two-and-a-half decades of violent conflict exacerbate the problem. Abuses by security forces continue. However, the government has worked to professionalize its army and police force. Increased oversight of police by internal and external monitors has helped to prevent some abuses, and human rights training has become a regular element for police and army personnel.

Reconstruction and Development

Setting the conditions necessary for economic growth is essential to long-term security and stability. Afghanistan has come a long way in seven years. Since 2001, Gross Domestic Product [a measure of a country's economic output], per capita income, and Foreign Direct Investment are all up. There has been considerable growth in Afghanistan's domestic revenues as well as international reserves, which have nearly doubled since 2004. However, Afghanistan still faces formidable economic challenges. The Afghan government remains overly dependent on foreign aid, with official revenues covering only 20 percent of recurrent costs. Costs, particularly for food and fuel, are rising, as is inflation. Access to credit is limited, and few Afghans are able to borrow.

Four strategic economic priorities support the counterinsurgency effort. These include: 1) embracing free market economic policy at senior levels of government, 2) enhancing government resources, 3) addressing inflation and 4) implementing structural reforms. Commitment to free markets means resisting costly subsidies and price controls that serve to reduce resources for other more constructive expenditures in areas like infrastructure, education, and healthcare. U.S. and international community efforts are assisting the Afghan government in moving towards a sustainable fiscal policy capable of generating revenue, managing resources, and operating without foreign financial support. The international community is also trying to boost economic growth by modernizing the country's infrastructure, particularly in the areas of electrical power, road construction, water management and agricultural development. Provincial Reconstruction Teams (PRTs) are key elements in these endeavors, ensuring that reconstruction and development efforts are coordinated at all levels and responsive to local needs. Finally, trade is benefiting, albeit slowly, from growing regional integration. Afghanistan is scheduled to join the South Asian Free Trade Area, bringing greater access to and integration with six other countries in the region including Bangladesh, Bhutan, India, Maldives, Nepal, Pakistan and Sri Lanka.

Looking Ahead

The U.S. commitment to Afghanistan is unwavering. Success in Afghanistan is both crucial to global security and is a moral responsibility. Achieving that success will take time, effort, resources, and the sustained interest and commitment of the international community.

Moreover, success will never be achieved through military means alone, but through a comprehensive approach that involves all elements of power: military, diplomatic, and economic. Above all, it will require a sustained effort to continue to develop the capacity of the Afghans themselves. Where we have begun to apply such an approach, real progress is being made. It is critical that we continue to build on the momentum that has been achieved.

Reconstruction Progresses in Afghanistan Despite Security Problems

John Metzler

John Metzler is a United Nations correspondent covering diplomatic and defense issues. He writes weekly for World Tribune.com, *a daily news service based in Washington, D.C., that specializes in the coverage of international affairs.*

Despite an upsurge in Islamic fundamentalist violence, a dangerously entrenched opium drug trade, and a reluctance of the international community to send additional troops to stem the Taliban [a fundamentalist Islamic militia] insurgency, the situation in Afghanistan has nonetheless seen some notable and impressive progress. Those gains emerged in a recent UN [United Nations] Security Council briefing on the embattled South Asian country, which is now six years into the still-uphill struggle for development and a more democratic government.

Progress Amid Insecurity

A Report on Afghanistan by UN Secretary General Ban Ki-moon stated that while most parts of the vast mountainous country remain stable, there's an increasingly coordinated insurgency in the south. Moreover, the conflict has been concentrated in a fairly small area where seventy percent of the security incidents were concentrated in ten percent of the districts. More worrying however were attacks on humanitarian workers and international relief staff. There's also been violence in Kabul the capital.

Most dangerously, the "Taliban and related armed groups and the drug economy represent fundamental threats to still

John Metzler, "Progress in Afghanistan Despite Ongoing Horrors, International Apathy," *WorldTribune.com*, March 20, 2008. Reproduced by permission.

fragile political, economic and social institutions. Despite tactical successes by national and international military forces, the anti-government elements are far from defeated."

First, some good news. United States UN Ambassador Zalmay Khalilzad, (himself an Afghan born American) stated, reconstruction has steadily increased. The extent of paved roads grew from 50 km in 2001 to 4,000 km today [2008]; the level of primary health care has increased from 8 percent coverage in 2001 to 80 percent today. The number of children enrolled in school increased from 900,000 in 2001 to more than 5 million today. He added, "Before virtually no girls were in school, today, about a third of all students are girls and young women." And even the economy has continued to grow at "impressive rates from 12-14 percent per year—the highest in South Asia."

Amb. Khalilzad concedes, "Security remains a huge challenge particularly in the southern provinces. The Afghan Ambassador Dr. Zahir Tanin admitted, "Providing security for our people is not only our main objective, but our primary challenge. Terrorists have increased attacks against civilians, schools, religious figures, security forces and international partners."

Reconstruction has steadily increased. The extent of paved roads grew ... the level of primary health care has increased ... [and] the number of children enrolled in school increased.

Obstacles to Economic Development

Following the overthrow of the fundamentalist Taliban forces in the wake of September 11, 2001, a robust international troop commitment has striven to bring progress and stability into a land of 30 million people which had become a terrorist state. On the security side there's the direct American troop commitment of 27,500 forces now being reinforced by 3,500 Marines. Equally there's a multinational mission with more than 40,000 troops from forty countries especially Australia, Britain, Canada, Germany, the Netherlands and Poland. The units are also involved in training missions for the Afghan army which today stands at 58,000 troops.

Yet the lingering dislocation and damage from the original Soviet occupation, (1979–89) followed by fundamentalist Taliban rule until 2001, serves as a millstone to socio-economic development. So does effective control of the vast and porous frontier with Pakistan which has been a primary conduit for terrorists and contraband. Amazingly, more than two million Afghan refugees are still living in Pakistan. The Pakistan government stresses that it has deployed 100,000 troops on the dangerous frontier as a contribution to control and counter-insurgency.

When it comes to major economic development it's countries like the USA, Canada, Japan and the European Union who are the global good guys.

When it comes to major economic development it's countries like the USA, Canada, Japan and the European Union who are the global good guys. This year [2008] Washington [that is, the United States] will provide $3 billion in total assistance including a billion dollars for health, education, and agriculture. Japan has given over $1.3 billion in assistance and has just announced a special package of $110 million for the border area. According to Tokyo's Ambassador Yukio Takasu, "Japan is fully committed to supporting the efforts of the government of and people of Afghanistan."

Still given the fluid security situation, the growing drug trade and the endemic problems with corruption and tribalism, it's a tough sell to get reluctant European governments to commit additional NATO [North Atlantic Treaty Organization, an alliance of European and North American countries] military forces into Afghanistan.

Australia's Ambassador Robert Hill stated it best, "I cannot stress enough that the international community has real and enduring interests in Afghanistan's stability. Afghanistan remains front-line in global efforts to defeat terrorism—a threat affecting all countries that support democracy, secularism and moderation. No member of the international community can afford to see Afghanistan succumb again to the forces of extremism and ideological fundamentalism."

There Is Progress in Afghanistan, But the Insurgent Danger Is Increasing

Paul Wells

Paul Wells is a Canadian journalist and pundit, currently work-ing as a columnist for Maclean's, *a Canadian current affairs magazine.*

The work of life and hope continues in Afghanistan. So does the work of unimaginable savagery. Each task has drawn practitioners of uncommon dedication. Even today, seven years into this mess, it is not clear who is winning. If victory has any decent meaning, we are nowhere close to be-ing able to claim it. And a very dangerous year lies just ahead. Afghans will elect a new government in 2009. The Taliban [a fundamentalist Islamic militia] and other insurgents will try to stop the voting. Drug lords will try to corrupt it. And a massive influx of American troops, perhaps 20,000 by 2010, will mark the arrival of a new American president determined to tip the balance of a stalemated war.

Even soldiers who eagerly await the arrival of U.S. rein-forcements worry about what will happen when they arrive. Many—though certainly not all—believe the level of violence will skyrocket in the short term and that the heart of the car-nage will be the country's south, including Kandahar [prov-ince], where most of the soldiers in the Canadian deployment are already stationed. It may be salutary violence; perhaps this war needs to get worse before it gets better. But one U.S. gen-eral put it this way.

"If you put three brigades in the heart of the Pashtun [an ethnic group in Afghanistan] south, the insurgents are gonna

Paul Wells, "There Is Progress in Afghanistan, But the Danger Is Increasing," *Macleans. ca*, December 18, 2008. Reproduced by permission.

come from Baluchistan [across the porous border in Pakistan], they're gonna come from far and wide. And you're going to see a level of violence that we have not seen in a long time. This is not the Taliban that we all know and love. You know, one little IED [improvised explosive device] takes a wheel off a vehicle, everybody gets bumped up but they're all okay. You're going to be seeing world-class IEDs. You're going to be seeing [rocket-propelled grenade] fire that is incredibly accurate. You're going to be seeing mortar fire that is incredibly accurate. And my belief is, you're going to see new weapons introduced into the theatre.". . .

Development work has markedly accelerated and there have been tentative steps toward better coordination. Roads are being paved, schools being built.

What a Difference a Year Makes

A year ago [2007], Afghanistan seemed to be at a crossroads. Western forces, increasingly supported by a homegrown Afghan army, were holding their own against insurgents, who were fighting a low-level guerrilla war of harassment against the Westerners and intimidation against local politicians. Development work was spotty and poorly coordinated. A year later it's as though the volume knob had been turned up on all of that.

Development work has markedly accelerated and there have been tentative steps toward better coordination. Roads are being paved, schools being built. Canada is distributing $1.2 million worth of wheat seed to 5,000 farmers so they might not have to plant opium poppies. Our government is financing the rebuilding of Sarpoza prison, the site of a spectacular and deadly prison break in June [2008], into perhaps the most secure and humane prison in Afghanistan. The professionalism and imagination of the Canadian public servants I met at the Provincial Reconstruction Team in Kandahar were a tonic for a journalistic refugee from the inanity of the coalition-government brinksmanship in Ottawa [Canada's capital].

Canada's civilian work in the south is led by Elissa Golberg, a loquacious career civil servant whose title—she is the first official "Representative of Canada in Kandahar "—is sewn in short form onto her body armour, as "THE ROCK." Soldiers are told to treat the Rock with the deference a general officer would get. She frets over her colleagues' safety, but she spends more time bumping along the dangerous roads around Kandahar than most other civilians.

Conversation about government services is slightly surreal because the roads are booby-trapped and the country is racked with insurgent violence.

Golberg has more discretion over her budgets than do many cabinet ministers in Ottawa. While she must account for her spending decisions, she is well clear of the leaden cloud of so-called "accountability" that most of today's Ottawa interprets to mean, "Don't do anything and you won't get into trouble." In Kandahar the cost of inaction is far too visible for such nonsense. Golberg will talk your ear off about wheat seed. Her enthusiasm is infectious.

One constant guideline for the Canadian civilians in Kandahar is to resist doing by themselves what they can goad or entice the Afghan government to do. This takes discipline. The Canadians have considerable resources, whereas getting and holding the Afghans' attention can be like trying to push string uphill. There will not always be Canadians in Kandahar, and before they leave they hope to instill some of the habits of a democratic government in Afghanistan's administration. Too much still rides on the personal attention of the local governor, who can be dedicated or corrupt. Rules and processes need to evolve so Afghans can depend on their government for basic services even if a third-rater is in charge.

And yet this whole conversation about government services is slightly surreal because the roads are booby-trapped and the country is racked with insurgent violence. Every single NGO [non-governmental organization] we met in Kandahar identified "security"—the local euphemism for war—as its primary challenge. Here too, last year's standoff between allies and insurgents seems to be holding, but at a higher level of carnage.

Increasing Violence

Abdul Rahim Wardak is Afghanistan's defence minister, a towering bear of a man who, 25 years ago, was fighting the Soviet occupiers alongside many of the mujaheddeen who became the insurgents he now combats. "Last year, in 2007, we thought we had experienced the bloodiest year ever," he said in his Kabul office. "But this year, unfortunately, the level of violence is 30 per cent to 40 per cent higher."

Wardak spent the first few years after the 2001 coalition invasion complaining that his Afghan National Army [ANA], which then stood at barely 10,000 undertrained troops with no modern equipment to speak of, could not ensure the country's security. As late as 2006 he was pleading for Western help to train a 150,000-strong Afghan army. Today he is nearly getting his wish: the ANA is on track to hit 86,000 soldiers by next year and 134,000 by 2011. Soldiers from NATO [North Atlantic Treaty Organization, an alliance of European and North American countries] countries rarely do anything now without their ANA colleagues. In 60 per cent of combined operations this year, Wardak said, the Afghans took the lead. "We have inflicted very heavy damage on the enemy leadership," he said.

But that is merely inciting the insurgents to more desperate measures, including the endemic use of roadside bombs that just killed six Canadians in eight days. And no matter how many insurgents the Afghan and Western troops kill or capture, more appear. Many come from Pakistan.

"I've got a 1,100-km open flank," said Maj.-Gen. Mart de Kruif, the newly arrived Dutch commander of Regional Command South, which includes Kandahar and the provinces on either side. The turbulent Pakistani elections a year ago, whose low point was the terrorist assassination of [Pakistan's former prime minister] Benazir Bhutto, took the Pakistani authorities' attention away from the border mountains for months. Almost inevitably, violence in Afghanistan's eastern and southern regions climbed.

NATO was slow to take an interest in the ANP's [Afghan National Police's] training.

In the last six months, NATO authorities in Afghanistan have tried to re-engage their Pakistani counterparts. When U.S. Gen. David McKiernan arrived in June [2008] to assume command of all NATO forces in Afghanistan, one of his first meetings was with Pakistan's chief of defence staff. Now they meet every month, and the two meet with the head of Afghanistan's army every two months. [Ron] Hoffman, the Canadian ambassador, has begun regular meetings with Randolph Mank, Canada's high commissioner in Islamabad [Pakistan's capital]. Len Edwards, the deputy minister of foreign affairs, was in Afghanistan when I was there. One item on his agenda was to begin coordinating a broader regional response to the Afghan conflict.

But open lines of communication can only accomplish so much. The Pakistani army's heavy-handed tactics make it ill-suited to fight a counterinsurgency. And most of the country's troops are on the eastern border with India, Pakistan's eternal nemesis. "It's not rocket science to know that if we can improve the relationship between India and Pakistan it will improve the situation here," de Kruif said. Unfortunately, the murderous attack on Mumbai by terrorists trained in Pakistan [November 26–29, 2008] is driving those countries' relationship in the other direction.

The Need for Police

In the meantime, the open border helps ensure that there will always be more bad guys than NATO and the Afghan army can handle. Someone else has to fill the gap. Ideally, somebody local who can spot suspicious behaviour by outsiders who, being Pashtun, are in most ways indistinguishable from the locals. "Police, police, police," Denis Thompson, the laconic Canadian brigadier-general who commands Joint Task Force Kandahar, said. "That's my number one worry. If you don't have the cops you can't hold the ground. And if you can't hold the ground you can't do anything else."

Traditionally, Afghan police were just an extension of local warlord clans, ill-equipped, unpaid except by bribes, and fabulously corrupt. On top of it all, since the insurgency began in 2002, Afghan National Police (ANP) officers have been the most vulnerable targets for attacks. More than 1,000 ANP officers have been killed this year [2008] alone.

NATO was slow to take an interest in the ANP's training. Some Western authorities still doubt the good faith of President Hamid Karzai's government in training the police. "You get all the Afghan leadership together, from Karzai on down," one senior NATO officer said. "Put 'em in Ghazi stadium [Kabul's main athletic venue] and ask them, 'Do you want a competent, professional, dedicated police force?' And give them some sort of truth serum. My guess is that fewer than 30 per cent of them would say yes. Shaking down a corrupt police force is how these guys make their money. People say, 'Clean up the police.' It's a cop-out. We need to clean up the government."

Despite that atmosphere of malign neglect, Western authorities have finally begun making strides toward training and professionalizing the police. One is salary reform: police are now paid at the same rate soldiers are, so taking bribes is no longer a necessity for simple survival. And they're now paid by electronic transfer using personalized smart cards—so the pay gets to the individual cop rather than to his boss or the local warlord.

Western authorities have finally begun making strides toward training and professionalizing the [Afghan] police.

The other big innovation is effective training. Western authorities wasted too many years training Afghan police one by one, teaching an officer new techniques—often beginning with basic literacy—and then sending him back to a corrupt and corrupting precinct station. Last year [2007] the westerners introduced Focused District Development [FDD], which trains every man in a police station together, while members of an elite national police squadron hold the fort in their absence. "Bring them in to train alone, they fail," one trainer said. "Bring the group in, even if you need to trim the group because of hot urinalysis and a couple of other problems, the rest of the group succeeds." Focused District Development is now key to a lot of other decisions about how to allocate resources in a theatre of war that's way too big for the NATO resources at hand. Military commanders now prefer not to clear an area of Taliban unless the police in that area have gone through FDD, because they're likeliest to be able to keep the Taliban out later.

In Kandahar, where many members of the ANP have been trained by members of Canadian police forces, Precinct 9 has doubled its rate of IED discovery this year. In Canada we only hear about IEDs when they kill our soldiers. But most victims of insurgent violence are Afghans. NATO soldiers hope the insurgents' shift from direct military conflict, which they can't win, to IEDs, which they can't target, will cost them local support. "The Taliban have lost ground with the local population," one soldier insists. "They don't deliver any services. The only service is, 'You pissed me off so I'm going to hang you from a lamp post.'"

But some Western authorities think even a U.S.-reinforced NATO contingent and a swiftly improving Afghan army and police corps won't be enough to end the standoff with the insurgents. That has some senior NATO officers mulling a dangerous and controversial option: recruiting and arming local tribal militias to help out. There is no formal plan along these lines, but we heard the option discussed at senior levels of the NATO leadership.

We also heard it contested, especially in the south, where tribal affiliations are infernally complex. Arming or paying one faction could have repercussions nobody could predict or control. "On a scale from smart to dumb," one officer said, holding his hands apart in front of him, "arming the tribes is over here." He nodded at the "dumb" end of his scale.

A Growing Challenge

If anything, it was harder after this trip to measure the room for optimism in Afghanistan than it was a year ago. The civilian and military resources Canada and its allies are deploying far exceed anything we have put to the task before. Reinforcements are on the way. But the challenge is growing too.

Meanwhile, soldiers keep dying. One of the many who have had to become authorities on that subject is Warrant Officer Colin Clansey. The compact, thoughtful 33-year-old believes he is the first bagpiper deployed to a combat theatre in that role by the Canadian Forces since the Second World War. Since only two soldiers at Kandahar Air Field know how to play the pipes—the other is a truck driver Clansey used to teach—they have been kept busy playing at the ramp ceremonies when transport aircraft fly soldiers' remains home. Not only to Canada, but to the U.S., Britain, Australia. Clansey has played at 25 ramp ceremonies in his nine months at Kandahar.

Soldiers from every country come, if their operational duties permit, to attend the ramp ceremonies. When the three who died on Dec. 5 [2008] went home, 2,000 of their comrades were on hand. Clansey sometimes plays Amazing Grace or songs associated with specific regiments, but this time he played a new song he wrote in November, Task Force Kandahar. "It's a funeral march, so it's very sombre at the start," he said. "But as it progresses, I tried to give it a more positive tone, so it has elements of hope and joy at the end. As if to express the hope that all this isn't in vain."

Inadequate and Inefficient Reconstruction Aid Is Undermining Progress in Afghanistan

National Security Network

National Security Network is a public policy organization that seeks to provide information about progressive national security solutions to policy makers and the public.

The long-term success of counter-terrorism efforts in Afghanistan means denying the country to Al Qaeda [an international terrorist network led by Osama bin Laden], the Taliban [a fundamentalist Islamic militia] and other extremist groups as a safe haven—which means helping the Afghan government become sufficiently stable, representative and effective that its citizens prefer it to the promises and threats of extremists.

As the fifth lowest ranking state on the UN [United Nations] Development Programme's Human Development Index, Afghanistan faces extraordinary challenges. Yet, considering the importance of the outcome, the U.S. contribution to reconstruction has been shockingly small. In constant dollars per capita, we have spent far less in Afghanistan than in Iraq—or in the Balkans in the 1990s. We have allowed the aid efforts to be poorly coordinated and riddled with waste—and funneled large amounts of the money back to American contractors rather than to Afghan agencies.

This failure is undermining the Karzai government [Hamid Karzai has been president of Afghanistan since December 7, 2004] and demoralizing Afghan civilians, making it easier for the Taliban insurgency to reestablish itself. A stronger Tali-

National Security Network, *Afghanistan Reconstruction: The Missing Link*, April 17, 2008. Reproduced by permission.

ban endangers our troops and poses a significant threat to all that we have achieved in Afghanistan. Washington [that is, the United States] must take care of our long-term security interests—and keep our promises to the Afghan people—by refocusing on Afghanistan, redoubling our assistance efforts, and addressing the problems of management and coordination on the ground.

The Situation in Afghanistan Is Grave

According to the Brookings Institution [a U.S. think tank], Afghanistan is the world's second weakest state. Not only did Afghanistan receive a worse rating than Iraq, but it is also the "most insecure" state, according to the Brookings Weak State Index. "It has suffered from a long history of violent conflict as well as a lack of government control over significant portions of its territory and an inability to curtail grave human rights abuses. In the area of social welfare, Afghanistan also receives the world's lowest score due to high child mortality, inadequate access to improved water and sanitation, and low primary school completion rates." [Brookings, 2/26/08]

Though we face greater challenges in Afghanistan than we did in any of the US engagements of the 1990s, reconstruction funding is shamefully absent.

Afghanistan received the 5th lowest rating on the 2007/2008 Human Development Index sponsored by UNDP [United Nations Development Programme]. It was ahead of only Burkina Faso, Mali, Sierra Leone and Niger. Its Human Poverty Index ratings are equally abysmal, and the United Nations Human Development Report for Afghanistan cites that in those terms, the country ranks as one of the "worst in the world." In addition, most Afghans live on less than a dollar a day, and infant mortality rates are among the world's highest, while life expectancy is extremely low. [Human Development Report for Afghanistan, 2007/2008]

Reconstruction Is a Low Priority

Though we face greater challenges in Afghanistan than we did in any of the US engagements of the 1990s, reconstruction funding is shamefully absent. "Afghanistan has received far less aid per capita since the U.S. invasion than any other post-conflict operation, such as those in Bosnia, Kosovo, or even Haiti. According to one Afghan expert, 'Aid per capita to Afghans in the first two years after the fall of the Taliban was around a tenth of that given to Bosnians following the end of the Balkan civil war in the mid-1990s.'" [Center for American Progress, 11/07]

Nearly half of the aid in Afghanistan is spent on consultants and contractors, and the Afghan government cannot account for an additional $5.3 billion.

Obstacles to rebuilding Afghanistan are huge, but Iraq is acting as a distraction and siphoning off resources. While Iraq has received a total of $34.2 billion in reconstruction funding over five years, Afghanistan by comparison has received just $11.5 billion over the more than seven years that U.S. forces have been on the ground and just $1.1 billion for 2008. [Congressional Research Service, 2/08].

The [George W. Bush] Administration has not been supportive enough of an internationally monitored trust fund, designed to [help] the Afghans build their capacity for good governance. "The fund is administered by the World Bank and supervised by a Management Committee consisting of the Asian Development Bank, the Islamic Development Bank, the World Bank, and the United Nations Development Program; it provides support for the Afghan government (including salaries, operations, and essential goods; and it funds national investment programs and projects). The United States has acknowledged the role of the Trust Fund, but has not given a significant portion of its money to it." [Center for American Progress, 11/07. World Bank]

Although the Administration calls Provincial Reconstruction Teams [PRTs] a critical tool for Afghan reconstruction, they receive less than five percent of the US assistance budget. PRTs are joint reconstruction teams that include military, development, and diplomatic personnel. "PRTs concentrate in three areas: governance, reconstruction and security." They engage in consultation with "provincial governors, police chiefs and elected provincial councils to increase capacity and improve the provision of services," support Provincial Development Councils, and engage in quick action village improvement projects following the withdrawal of Taliban insurgents. Despite these sweeping responsibilities, "less than five percent of the U.S. assistance budget is channeled through U.S. PRTs." [Jones-Pickering Report, 1/30/08]

Money Is Not Reaching People in Need

The relief effort has been poorly managed and inefficient. According to the Agency Coordinating Body for Afghan Relief, nearly half of the aid in Afghanistan is spent on consultants and contractors, and the Afghan government cannot account for an additional $5.3 billion. [Agency Coordinating Body for Afghan Relief, 3/24/08]

The Former World Bank Director in Kabul [Afghanistan's capital] described the amount of international aid wasted as intolerably high. "Jean Mazurelle, the former World Bank director in Kabul, has estimated that international aid wastage rates are between 35 and 40 percent, and has observed numerous instances of fraud and looting, often by private companies." Additional estimates are just as troubling—"Between problems with contractors, and the endemic corruption and graft in Afghanistan's government, U.S. and UK [United Kingdom] officials have estimated that up to half of international aid is siphoned off by corrupt police and tribal officials." [Center for American Progress, 11/07]

Much like the mission to secure the country, reconstruction programs in Afghanistan are poorly coordinated. Though there are 60 international donors to Afghanistan, their "programs to provide rural Afghans with alternative income sources remain underfunded and poorly coordinated. Each of NATO's [North Atlantic Treaty Organization, an alliance of European and North American countries] regional Afghan commands operates its own provincial reconstruction teams, and scores of nongovernmental organizations work in the country. But with few exceptions—such as Khost province under U.S. command in the east, where military and reconstruction resources are meshed—they share no overriding strategy or operational rules." [*Washington Post*, 1/14/08]

Ineffective Reconstruction Efforts Are Undermining the Afghan Government and Empowering the Taliban

Reconstruction failures have badly tarnished the Karzai government and created opportunities for the Taliban. "They [Afghans] are also increasingly frustrated with the failure of President Karzai's government to extend its authority and services throughout the country and by the lack of improvement in their daily lives six years after the international reconstruction process was launched. The Taliban have been able to exploit the Karzai government's shortcomings to their advantage." [Jones-Pickering Report, 1/30/08]

With few tangible benefits from reconstruction efforts, public support for the government is decreasing. In 2005, 77 percent of Afghans felt that their country was headed in the right direction, but today that number has dwindled to 54 percent. The Jones-Pickering Report suggests that a failure to address longstanding challenges stemming from "insecurity, weak governance, widespread corruption, a poor economy and unemployment" is at the core of declining Afghan support. [ABC News, 12/03/07, Jones-Pickering Report, 1/30/08]

Reconstruction failures have badly tarnished the Karzai government and created opportunities for the Taliban.

Failing to involve the Afghan government in the rebuilding of the country will result in diminished future capabilities. "According to Afghanistan's Finance Ministry, only 12 percent of the money from the international donor community for reconstruction and development projects was actually channeled through the Afghan government." This portends trouble, as "the current distribution of resources undermines comprehensive, long-term, effective planning and the ability of the Afghan government to provide services or establish its legitimacy." [Center for American Progress, 11/07]

Success Will Require That the United States Redouble Its Reconstruction Efforts

There can be no reconstruction without security and the United States must do more in this regard. "There is a need for more U.S. and international troops in Afghanistan. Afghanistan is larger in size and population than Iraq but has far fewer national and foreign troops." [Jones-Pickering Report, 1/30/08]

The United States should increase overall reconstruction assistance to Afghanistan. "The vast majority of U.S. funding in Afghanistan has gone to security. An additional $1 billion should be provided in non-military aid, contingent on greater transparency and accountability in U.S. assistance." [Center for American Progress, 11/07]

Enhance coordination of reconstruction initiatives. "Coordination between the Provincial Reconstruction Teams (PRT) is essential. Because most PRTs report directly back to national capitals, coordination among all the PRTs, with NGOs [nongovernmental organizations] and with the Karzai government is at best ad hoc. In fact, most PRTs are stove-piped back to national capitals and the ISAF [International Security Assistance Force, a group of NATO countries contributing to a peacekeeping mission in Afghanistan] commander has no ability to influence or coordinate their work. That must be corrected so that what happens in one province is related to both neighboring provinces as well as the national effort." [Atlantic Council, 1/31/08]

There can be no reconstruction without security and the United States must do more in this regard.

The Afghans must play a more active role in reconstruction to be perceived as legitimate. "The donor community should focus on giving the Afghan government credit for projects and programs. To do so, donors need to focus on improving Afghan government accounting and enhance anti-corruption reforms." In addition, development assistance must reach provinces soon after they rid themselves of the Taliban's presence, lest their inhabitants turn away from the fragile Afghan government. [Jones-Pickering Report, 1/30/08]

The PRT program must be strengthened across the board. "PRTs should reflect the strategic overview of U.S. and NATO efforts in Afghanistan and play an assigned role, tailored to the local circumstances. PRTs need an agreed [upon] concept of operations and basic common organizational structure as well as goals and objectives so they provide a standard range of services. They also need to coordinate among themselves on a regular basis (and not settle for quarterly conferences) to exchange ideas on "best practices." There is need for a common source of quick disbursing funds for PRTs, so they can support short and long-term development projects. PRTs need to provide information about their accomplishments to Afghans and the international community. There is also need for a set of metrics to evaluate PRT operations." [Jones-Pickering Report, 1/30/08]

The U.S. Invasion of Afghanistan Has Led to Millions of Unnecessary Deaths

Eric Walberg

Eric Walberg writes for Al-Ahram Weekly, *an English language weekly newspaper serving the Arab world.*

According to Gideon Polya, based on UNESCO [United Nations Educational, Scientific and Cultural Organization] data, the US invasion of Afghanistan has led to as many as 6.6 million unnecessary deaths. According to Washburn University law professor Liaquat Ali Khan, the "crime of genocide applies to the intentional killings that NATO [North Atlantic Treaty Organization, an alliance of European and North American countries] troops commit on a weekly basis in the poor villages and mute mountains of Afghanistan to destroy the Taliban." The occupation forces, which ironically include former Axis powers Germany and Japan, have created the New Auschwitz.

During a recent visit to Kabul [Afghanistan's capital] by US Secretary of State Condoleezza Rice, Afghan President Hamid Karzai defended his rule, saying the economy and education systems had improved and there was more democratic freedom under the new constitution. "It is not right that Afghanistan was forgotten," he said. Meaning, in diplo-speak, of course, it was, except by the drug-crazed bomber pilots, who made a record-breaking 3,572 bombing raids last year, 20 times the level two years earlier. But it has popped back into the news recently with a string of gloomy reports, a series of

Eric Walberg, "U.S. Invasion of Afghanistan Has Led to as Many as 6.6 Million Unnecessary Deaths," *The People's Voice*, February 15, 2008. Reproduced by permission of the author.

terrifying shoot-outs in Kabul, and a high-profile NATO meeting where words were had, and not pretty ones.

A Doomed NATO Occupation?

The invasion—well into its seventh year and approaching the 1979–88 Soviet nine-year occupation record—is increasingly being compared to the ill-fated British 19th century invasions, intended to undermine Russian influence in the so-called Great Game. Ironically, the current fiasco was similarly inspired by a Western desire to undermine Russian influence, and, taking a different and, as it turned out, extremely risky tack, began in 1979 to massively fund Osama bin Laden and other Muslim terrorists, something the 19th century Brits were not so foolhardy as to do. The result, of course, was the 2001 invasion and occupation, at first hailed as a new chapter for the hapless Afghans, but now seen as doomed, according to that pesky string of reports.

Armed resistance to foreign occupation is growing and spreading.

Paddy Ashdown, the US choice as United Nations "proconsul," "super-envoy," whatever, in Kabul, declared, "We are losing in Afghanistan." Quelle surprise, his appointment was vetoed by Karzai, who is desperately trying to portray himself as an independent leader of a country that has "turned the corner," despite the 6 million plus deaths and the recent tiff over British military policy in the south, which Karzai claims led to the return of the Taliban [a fundamentalist Islamic militia]. He complains that he was forced by the British to remove the governor of Helmand [province] with disastrous consequences, and was furious that, at the same time, Britain was secretly negotiating with the Taliban to set up "retirement camps" there for possible rebel defectors.

But then what should he expect? A US citizen and UNO-CAL oil executive, he was parachuted into Afghanistan when the Americans invaded in 2001 and confirmed in US-orchestrated elections three years later. Widely regarded as a US-British stooge, the "mayor of Kabul" surely remembers the fate of his pre-Taliban predecessor, Mohamed Najibullah, who spent four years in a UN [United Nations] basement in Kabul until liberated—castrated and hung from a lamp post by the Taliban in 1996.

A Growing Insurgency

Armed resistance to foreign occupation is growing and spreading. NATO figures show that attacks on Western and Afghan troops were up by almost a third last year [2007], to more than 9,000 "significant actions," the highest level since the invasion. Seventy percent of incidents took place in the southern Taliban heartland of Helmand, though the Senlis Council estimates that the Taliban now has a permanent presence in 54 per cent of Afghanistan, arguing that "the question now appears to be not if the Taliban will return to Kabul, but when." Watch out, Mr Karzai.

In addition to the 3,572 bombing raids in 2007, suicide bombings climbed to a record 140, compared to five between 2001 and 2005. The Taliban's base is increasingly the umbrella for a revived Pashtun [an ethnic sect in Afghanistan] nationalism on both sides of the Afghan-Pakistani border, as well as for jihadists and others committed to fighting foreign occupation. The UN estimates the Taliban have just 3,000 active fighters and about 7,000 part-timers, in contrast with more than 50,000 US and NATO troops. Their command structure is diffuse and when it comes to guerrilla tactics—suicide attacks, roadside bombs, kidnapping and assassination—the militants have become frighteningly proficient.

"Make no mistake, NATO is not winning in Afghanistan," said a report issued 30 January [2008] by the Atlantic Council of the United States, chaired by retired General James Jones, who until 2006 served as the supreme allied commander of NATO in Afghanistan. "It remains a failing state. It could become a failed state," warned the report, which called for "urgent action" to overhaul NATO strategy in coming weeks before an anticipated new offensive by Taliban insurgents in the spring.

Kabul, relatively incident-free in the first two years after the removal of the Taliban, now sees regular rocket attacks, kidnappings, explosions and suicide bombings.

The Afghanistan Study Group, created by the Center for the Study of the Presidency, which was also involved with the Iraq Study Group, concluded, "the United States and the international community have tried to win the struggle in Afghanistan with too few military forces and insufficient economic aid," and lack a clear strategy to "fill the power vacuum outside Kabul and counter the combined challenges of reconstituted Taliban and Al-Qaeda forces in Afghanistan and Pakistan, a runaway opium economy, and the stark poverty faced by most Afghans."

Whoa. Did it ever occur to these think-tankers that just maybe they can never "win"? That the US invaded Afghanistan illegally, and the Taliban, still the legitimate government there, will continue to battle on, to wait it out, no matter how many bombs and dollars the US et al throw at it?

As if these reports aren't enough for the frazzled president, on 15 January [2008] rebels attacked Kabul's posh five-star Serena Hotel, targeting the ex-pat elite in the most fortified site in the capital, killing seven guests and staff. This was no straightforward suicide bombing, but an armed attack which allowed the gunmen to carry out a shooting spree before they were stopped, the one phenomenon security agencies have no defence against. Kabul, relatively incident-free in the first two years after the removal of the Taliban, now sees regular rocket attacks, shootings, kidnappings, explosions and suicide bombings.

A few weeks after Serena, Kabul witnessed dozens of armed police laying siege to the house of Uzbek warlord and Chief of Staff to the Afghan commander-in-chief General Abdul-Rashid Dostum, in the heart of the diplomatic district, after 50 of his followers abducted political rival Akbar Bai and several others, beating them to a pulp. "This is a conspiracy by the government against General Dostum," loyalist Mohamed Alim Sayee said. "If any harm occurs to Dostum, seven to eight provinces will turn against the government." Watch out, Mr Karzai.

Cracks in the NATO Coalition

Major cracks are appearing every day, and not only in the statues of the Bamyan Buddha, but in impregnable fortress-NATO, the latest triggered by America's closest ally Canada. It set off the current crisis by threatening to withdraw all its troops this year [2008] unless other NATO members could be conned into deploying troops in the dangerous southern province of Kandahar, where in a brief two years, Canada lost 80 of its 2,500 troops, its highest casualty rate since native tribes were mowed down in the 19th century by the British army. This tantrum forced an emergency NATO meeting . . . 7–8 February [2008], to be followed by a summit in—yes—Romania in April [2008]. US generals meeting deep in Eastern Europe pushing Western Europeans to cough up troops for Central Asia. Most interesting.

Setting the stage the day before his junket to an obscure country which just happens to border Russia, US Secretary of Defense Robert Gates told the House Armed Services Committee that the alliance could split into countries that were "willing to fight and die to protect people's security and those who were not. You can't have some allies whose sons and daughters die in combat and other allies who are shielded from that kind of a sacrifice."

Did this blackmail work? Did Germany, Britain, Poland et al cough up? In the UK [United Kingdom], 62 percent want all 7,800 troops withdrawn within a year. Similar polling results keep German Chancellor Angela Merkel from signing on the dotted line. She said it would send around 200 combat soldiers to north Afghanistan but no way would she bail out the Canadians. In Paris, a spokesman for [French] President Nicolas Sarkozy did not confirm reports that 700 paratroopers could go to the south. The Polish chief of the defence staff said the government is considering increasing their forces, despite being elected only last October [2007] expressly on a policy of bringing its troops home from Iraq and, presumably, Afghanistan. Only the US itself made any real effort to mollify the Canadians, agreeing to deploy 3,200 US Marines temporarily, but warning that the others must come through before the end of the year. Stay tuned.

Even the early limited gains for women and girls in some urban areas are now being reversed, offset by an explosion of rape and violence against women.

At the love-in in Lithuania, Gates softened his undiplomatic language somewhat: "I don't think that there's a crisis, that there's a risk of failure." Which, in diplo-speak of course means there is a crisis, etc. Gates also squelched early suggestions that the US would take over command of combat operations in southern Afghanistan. "I don't think that's realistic any time soon," Gates said. Why bother? At present, an American four-star general is in overall command of the NATO mission. Americans are in command of the regional mission in eastern Afghanistan, while a Canadian is in command of the south.

"I worry that for many Europeans the missions in Iraq and Afghanistan are confused," Gates said as he flew to Munich to deliver a speech at an international security conference 10 February. "Many of them, I think, have a problem with our involvement in Iraq and project that to Afghanistan and do not understand the very different—for them—the very different kind of threat." But wait! The US coordinator on Iraq, David Satterfield, suggested only last month that Iraq would turn out to be America's "good war," while Afghanistan was going "bad." Can't these guys get their stories straight? Which is it, Mr Gates? Is good bad? Or is bad good? Just maybe bad is bad? Is that too hard to believe?

The original aims of the US-led invasion were the capture of Mullah Omar, the Taliban leader, and Osama bin Laden, along with the destruction of Al-Qaeda [an international terrorist network led by bin Laden]. None of those aims has been achieved. Instead, the two leaders remain free, while Al-Qaeda has spread from its Afghan base into Pakistan, Iraq and elsewhere, and Afghanistan has become the heroin capital of the world. For the majority of Afghans, occupation has meant the exchange of obscurantist theocrats for brutal and corrupt warlords, rampant torture and insecurity, depleted uranium bombing and the 6.6 million deaths—all thanks to Western altruism. Even the early limited gains for women and girls in some urban areas are now being reversed, offset by an explosion of rape and violence against women.

What we see is a classic case of blowback. With the decision to expand NATO and use it as its proxy in illegal invasions after the collapse of the Soviet Union—notably Iraq, Serbia, Afghanistan and again Iraq—instead of dissolving it, the West is merely reaping its whirlwind in the form of unending war and now internal squabbles.

"Events in Afghanistan have become a motor for the transformation of the alliance," said a senior NATO diplomat. In fact, the collapse of Afghanistan is just another domino in a long line since the "victory over Communism." "Fail" a state and what do you get? The resurgence of Pashtun nationalism in southern Afghanistan and northern Pakistan, just like in the soon-to-be republics of Kosovo and Kurdistan. Long live independent Pashtunistan!

Will NATO bombs soon be raining down on Islamabad, demanding that Pakistan allow the heroic, suffering Pashtuns to unite with their brothers in a just liberation struggle? God knows there are Pashtun guerrilla groups who, like their Kosovan and Kurd soulmates, would eagerly accept US/NATO arms and protection. After all, the US once generously equipped them with Stinger missiles in their struggle to "liberate" Afghanistan.

The lack of troops means heavy reliance on air power with its concomitant "collateral damage," a euphemism for killing civilians.

Afghanistan in a Nutshell

- Policies of the "international community" put immediate gains and Western interests before sustainable goals. In security, US Operation Enduring Freedom focused solely on routing the Taliban and Al-Qaeda, while NATO forces were confined largely to Kabul. Not until 2004 was security for the country considered. Even now, security operations in the country are compartmentalised into three distinct and uncoordinated areas, resulting in confusion and controversy. The global "war against terror" is conducted by US-led Coalition Forces; the counter-insurgency war is waged by the NATO-led International Security Assistance Force; the war against drugs is led by the Afghan police.

- The lack of troops means heavy reliance on air power with its concomitant "collateral damage," a euphemism for killing civilians.

- Instead of creating a strong national army and police force, occupiers now endorse the rearming of communities through the "auxiliary police," a euphemism for rearming the very warlords they spent five years trying to disarm.

- Relations with the Taliban follow the pendulum principle. All dissenters are lumped with the Taliban and policy swings between making peace with the Taliban to deporting those who dare talk to them, as the recent retirement camp scandal and deportation of German diplomats in December 2007 reveal.

- The 2004 constitution established a strong presidential system, stoking tensions in a war-torn state with tribal divisions, putting too much formal power in the hands of the winner, who has heavy responsibilities but little real authority, creating a breeding ground of nepotism and corruption. Karzai relies heavily on his Northern Alliance Tajik and Uzbek comrades, who make up 27 and 10 percent of the population respectively, though Karzai is nominally Pashtun, the largest ethnic group. A more inclusive parliamentary system of government, with a ceremonial president or king and stronger local and regional governments, might help, though this would most likely just accelerate the present collapse of all central government and the return of warlord anarchy. At present, Karzai really only answers to a fractious cluster of foreign donors.

- Finally there is the one flourishing industry—opium and marijuana production. Opium production was up 34 percent last year, 10 percent of proceeds being tithed by the Taliban. Worse yet, it is not at all clear whether this is good or bad from a Western point of view, despite loud protestations about the evils of drugs. It is well documented that many governments in the region, not to mention the CIA, are deeply involved in both sides of the so-called war on drugs. The Taliban actually wiped out all drug production in 2000. Some critics of US foreign policy argue that the 2001 invasion was actually prompted by a distaste for this successful campaign, which led to a crisis in the European drug black-market.

Ongoing Military Operations Have Displaced and Impoverished Afghan Citizens

Mohammed Daud Miraki

Mohammed Daud Miraki is a social scientist with expertise in Afghanistan, public policy, urban planning, international development, political science, and Middle Eastern Studies. He is the author of Afghanistan After "Democracy": The Untold Story through Photographic Images, *from which this article is excerpted.*

After the invasion of Afghanistan in October 2001, the rhetoric of democracy, "liberation" and reconstruction echoed from the official White House propaganda machine, neo-conservatives and conservative media outlets. This rhetoric, supported by the influx of billions of dollars, has not only failed to bring about reconstruction, it has made life difficult for the ordinary Afghan people and subjected future generations to a perpetual suffering and death.

U.S. Propaganda About Afghanistan

Meanwhile, as the US government was preparing to invade Afghanistan, it launched a barrage of rhetoric and propaganda, aimed at convincing the world that its goals were to "liberate" Afghanistan, free Afghan women and children, and rebuild schools. While President [George W.] Bush talked about a plan equal in scope to the Post WWII Marshall plan [the European Recovery Program, instituted in 1947 to rebuild Europe after World War II], my relatives and friend gave me a different view of reality: US bombs raining down in the night while they slept. This sickened me, and I told my parents: "Our blood is cheap. First, it is spilled by the Russians. Now it is the Americans' turn." Like all mothers across the world who are protective, my mother told me, "Son, leave everything to God. Don't talk about these issues. People are put in prison as we speak." My father, a General in the Afghan Intelligence Service when we left the country in 1982, replied, "This is a tragedy, but you have to tell the truth and expose the lies that are bleeding our people."

Before and after the invasion the Bush administration's rhetoric and propaganda was shameless. One of the biggest issues it abused was women's rights. Karen Hughes of the Bush administration led the Coalition Information Center (CIC) to spread lies about the Bush administration's intentions. Laura Bush took her turn and made the following shocking accusation on November 17, 2001, in her husband's weekly radio address from their ranch in Crawford, Texas: "Only the terrorists and the Taliban threaten to pull out women's fingernails for wearing nail polish." British Prime Minister Tony Blair, also known as "Bush's Poodle," repeated Laura Bush's accusations three days later: "In Afghanistan, if you wear nail polish, you could have your nails torn out."

In reality, however, Afghan women were being killed, losing their family members and homes thanks to the US's "liberation" bombing. In early October, an Afghan woman, Nurgessa, who roamed the deserted streets of Kandahar accompanied by her little boy, said the following about the "liberation":

Last night, while we were sleeping the Americans bombed our homes. When I woke up I saw Agha Gul [her husband] shattered into pieces and my other two sons had their heads blown away, I screamed for my little boy, Sa'may. Sa'may was unconscious. I ran while the bombs were dropping. This morning I woke up with my little Sa'may looking for grass. I want to boil grass for Sa'may because he is hungry. We have nothing left. Sa'may's father and my other beautiful sons were all that I had.

The UK [United Kingdom] *Guardian* reported the pain and misery imposed on women in Afghanistan on October 7, 2002, a year after the US invasion:

Few people paid a higher price when America's military machine launched its war in Afghanistan a year ago today than Orfa. She was away visiting relatives when the American fighter jet dropped out of the clear midday sky and dived towards her village in the hills outside Kabul. When she returned home a few days later it was left to her neighbours to explain the inexplicable. They told her that the aircraft, almost certainly an F-16, had mistakenly fired a precision Mk 82 500lb bomb directly at her small mud and stone house, killing her husband, carpet weaver Gul Ahmad, his second wife, five of their daughters and one son. Two children from the house next door also died. When the *Guardian* first found Orfa last year, four weeks after the bombing, she was still deep in shock, haunted by the horrifying image of her family's remains. Their bodies were so badly torn apart they could not be identified for separate graves.

The report continues:

'I don't know how long it will be now until the Americans help us,' Orfa, 32, said. 'They have done nothing for us and I don't know what to do with my children or how to support them.' The awkward truth is that the only outside help Orfa has received has come from the visitors who arrived at Bibi Mahru the day after the bombing. They were Taliban officials still clinging to power in the dying days of the ultra-orthodox Islamist regime and they brought shrouds for the dead as well as 17,000 Pakistan rupees (£190). Orfa shared the Taliban's money with her next-door neighbour, whose two children were killed by the same bomb. Most of her portion went on medical care for her seriously injured and deeply disturbed son, Jawad, 14. 'He went to his father's grave every day and just stood there staring it at. I don't have any more money to spend on medical care for him,' she said. Now the boy has been sent to Pakistan with an aunt in an attempt to break his grief-stricken obsession.

Afghan women were being killed, losing their family members and homes thanks to the US's "liberation" bombing.

The pain and suffering of these women were of no consequence for Laura Bush when she proudly stated the following only five weeks after October 7, 2001: "Because of our recent military gains in much of Afghanistan, women are no longer imprisoned in their homes. The fight against terrorism is also a fight for the rights and dignity of women."

Reconstruction: The Everlasting Illusion

When the false promise of hope is dangled to desperate people, it is natural that they are euphoric at being saved by the mighty rich United States from misery, hunger and homelessness. However, nothing could be farther from the truth. In fact, the so-called reconstruction is nothing but an unreachable, illusive carrot dangled from a distance away that gets farther with every passing day.

The so-called reconstruction is a hollow dream that has turned into a nightmare more terrifying as time goes on. Not only has it created social ills and infested Afghan society beyond repair; it has also failed to create anything tangible. The problem is rooted mostly in development aid, which never fulfills its promise. Furthermore, reconstruction cannot succeed when it is only a foreign policy instrument and talking points in speeches of George [W.] Bush and others glorifying this deception as inevitable success.

The classic Western models of success: elections, representative governments, parliament do not mean anything to the common man and woman of the Afghan society. These people were eager for an avenue of survival and hope for the future. The following statement from a poor resident of Kabul sums up the failure of the US-led reconstruction program and the hoopla it has created and resonated from the Western corporate media outlets: "Election, parliament and constitution? What can I do with that? Can I eat, wear and support my children with these symbols? No, I cannot. I am a widow. I care about survival, food and shelter for my children." . . .

The so-called reconstruction is nothing but an unreachable, illusive carrot dangled from a distance away that gets farther with every passing day.

Failures of Development Aid

The US and other Western governments pursued development aid as their tool of foreign policy without taking into account the needs of Afghan people and the position of the Afghan government. The practices of the donor nations not only undermined the government's legitimacy by bypassing its authority, but they also did little to improve the future of the Afghan people, who are still wondering where the money went.

The problem with the US-led reconstruction aid has been two-fold, counter-narcotics and antiterrorism campaigns and distribution of aid is done outside the mechanism of the Afghan government.

First, it advanced US foreign policy goals. Two basic policy goals have been pursued. They were counter narcotics and anti-terrorism campaigns because the US-led coalition viewed security in militaristic terms only. The pursuit to eradicate poppy cultivation went hand in hand with the anti-insurgency operations. In both cases, they undermined the stability of Afghan society by contributing to poverty and perpetual underdevelopment.

The counter-narcotics measure or war on drugs has not only failed in the US but also in South America and Asia.

However, since the collapse of [the] Taliban was partly facilitated by the assistance of former drug barons, naturally those drug dealers resorted to their old ways. Drought, lack of humanitarian assistance and failure to provide alternative crops has led farmers to cultivate poppies so they can survive. The UK and US pursued the war on drugs . . . without considering poor farmers' sustenance. Instead of addressing the basic needs of the Afghan people, the international community resorted to its own short sighted policy goals. How could they now eradicate opium when their allies during the invasion in 2001 were drug dealers and other organized criminals? Perhaps, the rhetoric was for publicity purposes and the constituency at home. [Former British prime minister] Tony Blair was lying blatantly when he said that the coalition forces would destroy Taliban-controlled poppy fields. However, Blair has conveniently forgotten that the Bush administration had awarded the Taliban regime $43 million in 2001 for eradicating opium poppy cultivation in Afghanistan.

If the invaders—Americans and British—had met the basic needs of the Afghan people, stability would have been more likely than the current state of affairs. . . .

By the same token, the pursuit of the War on Terror on a military front has further alienated the Afghan people and revealed the US invasion for what it really is: a campaign to ensure US security and global geo-strategic hegemony [domination].

If the invaders—Americans and British—had met the basic needs of the Afghan people, stability would have been more likely than the current state of affairs.

Where the most effective, long lasting effects would be the eradication of conditions that foster extremism, military operations have been chosen over poverty eradication and development. . . .

Moreover, the maltreatment of individuals detained by the US-led coalition has further angered Afghans. Some of the horror stories of abuse committed by the US military circulated throughout Afghanistan and have contributed to the perception of the population that the US forces are evil.

Once families have been terrorized by military forces and sustained losses, they abandon their villages only to be terrorized by abject poverty, hopelessness and disease.

Ongoing military operations have contributed to mass displacement of population in Southern and Southwestern Afghanistan. Villagers displaced by vicious military campaigns have created rudimentary refugee camps where hundreds of children and elderly die on [a] daily basis. Furthermore, the continued loss of life caused by these military campaigns exacerbates the situation. Once families have been terrorized by military forces and sustained losses, they abandon their villages only to be terrorized by abject poverty, hopelessness and disease. The hopelessness and sheer terror of poverty and disease is illustrated by the following quote from a villager in Kandahar: "Democracy is important according to your culture but according to our culture feeding our children is more important."

Flawed Aid Distribution

The second problem with the US-led reconstruction has been the flawed method of aid distribution. The distribution of aid through alternative mechanisms—Non-governmental Organizations (NGOs) and UN [United Nations] agencies—and the imposition of restrictions on development aid, the USAID [U.S. Agency for International Development] undermined the legitimacy of the Afghan government to its population, which added to the total failure of this concoction called reconstruction.

The Afghan government would have been the most cost-effective way to pursue development projects. Instead, 3 quarters of the development aid is channeled through NGOs, consulting firms and UN agencies. This fact is reported in the recent World Bank report quoting World Bank Economist William Byrd, who co-authored the report: "Roughly three quarters of total aid to Afghanistan goes outside government channels."

It continues:

> Our report emphasizes that this is a very serious problem for aid management, aid effectiveness and achieving results for the Afghan people. Aid going outside government channels sometimes can be delivered quickly, but is often at a very high cost and does not help the government build its capacity to oversee the delivery of services itself. . . .

This undermines the legitimacy of the Afghan government, a fact also reiterated by the World Bank Country Director Alastair McKechnie: "Furthermore, the credibility of the government is increased as it demonstrates its ability to oversee services and become accountable for results to its people and the newly elected parliament." The Director continued, "In Afghanistan the wastage of aid is sky-high; there is real looting going on, mainly by private enterprises. It is a scandal . . . In 30 years of my career I have never seen anything like it."

Billions of dollars have been wasted without truly rebuilding.

McKechnie's statement is not surprising since 47% of the US development budget is wasted on over-priced and lavish technical assistance. That is why Afghan Ministries are flooded with over-priced experts, expatriates, USAID-funded organizations and consulting firms. This business model of micro management leads countries like Afghanistan to lack confidence in the "aid" that they are receiving. . . .

The Afghan Ministry of Finance has to wait for "approval" from international donors to determine the appropriate venue of spending. Due to the intrusive nature of the donor institutions, the Afghan Finance Ministry is unable to raise the salary for Afghan civil servants. The ministry proposed increases in salary for government employees to enable them to sustain themselves in light of the massive cost of living increases. Unfortunately, the IMF [International Monetary Fund] rejected the proposal, thereby facilitating the continued cycle of poverty and corruption. Only recently has there been agreement from the World Bank on the increase of salary for civil servants. This type of intrusive approach undermines local perception of need imposed by what the donor considers to be the appropriate avenue. . . .

The intimate relationship of large for-profit organizations and the USAID result in the allocation of reconstruction contracts to companies, most of which are politically connected. Journalist and photographer Ann Jones describes the cozy relationship between the USAID and contractors:

> Sometimes it invites only one contractor to apply, the same efficient procedure that made Halliburton so notorious and profitable in Iraq. In many fields it "pre-selects vendors" by accepting bids every five years or so on an IQC—that's an "Indefinite Quantities Contract". Contractors submit indefinite information about what they might be prepared to do in unspecified areas, should some more definite contract materialize; the winners become designated contractors who are invited to apply when the real thing comes along. US-AID generates the real thing in the form of an RFP, a Request for Proposals, issued to the "pre-selected vendors" who then compete (or collaborate) to do—in yet another country—work dreamed up in Washington by theoreticians unencumbered by first-hand knowledge of the hapless "target". . . .

Unfortunately, billions of dollars have been wasted without truly rebuilding:

During 2002–5, the U.S. spent about $1.3 billion—or some 38 percent of the total $3.6 billion pledged by the international donor community after 2001—on Afghan reconstruction (as compared to $30 billion in Iraq), that is, a little over $250 million per year, a paltry amount. Moreover, the Bush administration has [reduced] reconstruction aid to Afghanistan from $1 billion in 2005 to $623 million in 2006. Afghans are widely . . . reported to being increasingly disenchanted with the U.S.-led reconstruction program. Projects languish unfinished, and project quality leaves much to be desired. For example the USAID in 2004 budgeted to build or renovate 289 schools, but U.S. contractors built only eight and refurbished 77, according to the U.S. Government Accountability Office (GAO). Likewise, the USAID budgeted to build or rehabilitate 253 health clinics in Afghanistan; eight were built and none were rehabilitated. The GAO pointed to poor contractor performance (and security problems, inconsistent financing, staff shortages, lack of oversight). Other reports echo the concern over the poor quality of work undertaken. For example, in a village close to the U.S. occupation forces' main base at Bagram, a mud-brick school built in 2003 compliments of American taxpayers is now in utter disrepair—its walls crumbling and its roof pitted by termites chewing into untreated wooden beams. Moreover, the project costs of official U.S.-sponsored projects are often much higher than by a private NGO. For example, CARE International built 40 schools in 2004, which in most cases cost $10,000–$20,000 less than U.S-sponsored projects. . . .

So how much have Afghans benefited from the US imposed democracy and reconstruction?

The short answer is not much.

The Lack of Progress in Afghanistan Has Allowed the Taliban to Return to the Country

International Council on Security and Development

The International Council on Security and Development (ICOS) is an international think tank that focuses on global security, public security, public health, and drug control.

While the international community's prospects in Afghanistan have never been bleaker, the Taliban [a fundamentalist Islamic militia] has been experiencing a renaissance that has gained momentum since 2005. At the end of 2001, uprooted from its strongholds and with its critical mass shattered, it was viewed as a spent force. It was naively assumed by the US and its allies that the factors which propelled the Taliban to prominence in Afghanistan would become moribund in parallel to its expulsion from the country. The logic ran that as ordinary Afghans became aware of the superiority of a western democratic model and the benefits of that system flowed down to every corner of the country, then the Taliban's rule would be consigned to the margins of Afghan history.

However, as seven years of missed opportunity have rolled by, the Taliban has rooted itself across increasing swathes of Afghan territory. According to research undertaken by ICOS [International Council on Security and Development, a policy think tank] throughout 2008, the Taliban now has a permanent presence in 72% of the country. This figure is up from 54% in November 2007, as outlined in the ICOS report *Stum-*

International Council on Security and Development, *Struggle for Kabul: The Taliban Advance*. London, United Kingdom: International Council on Security and Development, 2008. Reproduced by permission.

bling into Chaos: Afghanistan on the Brink. Moreover, it is now seen as the de facto governing power in a number of southern towns and villages. The increase in their geographic spread illustrates that the Taliban's political, military and economic strategies are now more successful than the West's in Afghanistan. Confident in their expansion beyond the rural south, the Taliban is at the gates of the capital and infiltrating the city at will.

Closing in on Kabul

Of the four doors leading out of Kabul [Afghanistan's capital], three are now compromised by Taliban activity. The roads to the west, towards the Afghan National Ring Road through Wardak to Kandahar become unsafe for Afghan or international travel by the time travellers reach the entrance to Wardak province, which is about thirty minutes from the city limits. The road south to Logar is no longer safe for Afghan or international travel. The road east to Jalalabad is not safe for Afghan or international travel once travellers reach the Sarobi Junction which is about an hour outside of the city. Of the two roads leaving the city to the north only one—the road towards the Panjshir valley, Salang tunnel and Mazar—is considered safe for Afghan and international travel. The second road towards the north which leads to the Bagram Air Base is frequently used by foreign and military convoys and subject to insurgent attacks.

By blocking the doors to the city in this way, the Taliban insurgents are closing a noose around the city and establishing bases close to the city from which to launch attacks inside it. Using these bases, the Taliban and insurgent attacks in Kabul have increased dramatically—including kidnapping of Afghans and foreigners, various bomb attacks and assassinations. This dynamic has created a fertile environment for criminal activity. The links between the Taliban and criminals are increasing and the lines between the various violent actors becoming blurred. All of these Taliban successes are forcing the Afghan government and the West to the negotiating table.

The Taliban's unity of purpose gives it a distinct edge over the cumbersome command structure of Western security and development efforts.

The Taliban in Control

The Taliban are now dictating terms in Afghanistan, both politically and militarily. At the national level, talk of reconciliation and power sharing between undefined moderate elements of the Taliban movement and elected government officials is commonplace. At a local level, the Taliban are manoeuvring skilfully to fill the governance void, frequently offering a mellower version of localised leadership than characterised their last stint in power.

Simultaneously, the asymmetric threat posed by agile Taliban forces to NATO's [North Atlantic Treaty Organization, an alliance of European and North American countries] ill-equipped, lumbering military machine ensures that genuine security cannot be established in any of the 72% of Afghan territory where the Taliban has a permanent presence. Without appropriate resources at their disposal, NATO is not prepared for the challenge. Indeed, any real difference would require a significant troop increase numbering in the tens of thousands. It is the combination of recruitment bulk and propaganda know-how that enables the Taliban to outlast NATO-ISAF [International Security Assistance Force] and US forces. Simplistic though it may be, the Taliban's unity of purpose gives it a distinct edge over the cumbersome command structure of Western security and development efforts.

Over the past three years, ICOS' research and analysis portfolio has catalogued a series of mistakes made by the international community in the quest to pacify the insurgency.

There have been some signs of progress, such as opening the international debate on sending more troops, but also a stubborn adherence to failing policies such as military actions leading to civilian casualties, lack of effective aid and development, and support for aggressive poppy crop eradication programmes.

The inability of domestic and international actors to counter the entrenchment of the insurgency in Afghanistan is deeply troubling, and the failure of NATO's political masters to address the realities of the security situation in Afghanistan has taken the country and the [Hamid] Karzai government to a precipice. It will take more than a military defeat of the Taliban to build trust, especially in the southern provinces.

The Taliban has managed to spread instability across large parts of Afghanistan through a sustained campaign of violence.

The insurgency continues to turn NATO's weaknesses into its own strengths. Until external actors expand focus beyond the military dimensions, by targeting needs at a grassroots level and thus restoring its previous levels of support, there is a danger that Afghanistan will be lost for at least another generation. . . .

Secrets of the Taliban Success

The Taliban's success can largely be attributed to its use of a wide array of asymmetric measures aimed at negating NATO's technical military superiority. Drawing on a sophisticated array of terror tactics and a complex intelligence network, the Taliban has managed to spread instability across large parts of Afghanistan through a sustained campaign of violence. With kidnappings and bombings increasingly commonplace even in Kabul itself, the war is now being fought not just in the country's fringes, but at its heart. A series of recent attacks, such as the audacious Kandahar jailbreak in June 2008, have also boosted the organisation's prestige and indicated their ability to evade detection by Afghan and Western intelligence networks.

Crucially, the Taliban appears to be also winning on another front—the battle for hearts and minds. By tapping into a variety of local grievances against NATO-ISAF and the Kabul government, from poppy eradication and bombing leading to civilian casualties, to high levels of unemployment and chronic underdevelopment despite billions of dollars of aid, the insurgency has succeeded in attracting sympathy beyond its traditional support base and gained a measure of political legitimacy among many Afghans.

This was already apparent in 2007, when ICOS conducted an opinion survey to assess local perceptions of the Taliban and its propaganda campaign. Highlighting a growing lack of faith in NATO and the Afghan government, almost half of all respondents doubted their ability to achieve a decisive victory, and more than a quarter of those interviewed expressed their support for the Taliban.

Crucially, the Taliban appears to be also winning on another front—the battle for hearts and minds.

International Failures

Underlying this expansion of Taliban presence is the international community's failure to deliver on the many promises of a better life made to the Afghan people in the wake of the invasion. Seven years on, much of the country still lacks basic amenities and the majority of the population struggle to secure necessities such as food and shelter, let alone a sustainable livelihood. Field research by ICOS has presented a picture of acute hardship and deep uncertainty, with the majority of respondents worried about feeding their families.

Economic outreach to Afghans at a grassroots level, through livelihood creation and microfinance schemes, remain central elements of a successful strategy. Yet developmental expenditure continues to be dwarfed by military spending, resulting in an 'expectations gap' that the insurgency has been able to exploit. The Taliban has managed to make a manifesto out of the shortcomings of the international community and the Afghan government. Even the West's failure to prevent the rise of terrorist violence in the country has paradoxically helped the Taliban present itself in some areas as a provider of law and order, despite its responsibility for the ongoing instability.

The international community's failure to give sufficient focus to the needs and desires of the Afghan population and channel them into effective policy responses is a key aspect of the insurgency's rising popularity.

Despite the vast injections of international capital flowing into the country . . . the state is once again in serious danger of falling into the hands of the Taliban.

The Opium Issue

This is particularly true of the current approach to tackling Afghanistan's endemic opium production. A key element of present policy is eradication, which invariably drives farming communities away from the West and into the arms of the Taliban. ICOS suggests an alternative proposal called Poppy for Medicine, which would license some of Afghanistan's cultivation of opium for conversion into morphine.

If implemented, this proposal would provide poppy growers with the chance to channel their harvest legally into the global morphine market. The current policy of forced poppy crop eradication, on the other hand, destroys their source of income without providing them with an alternative livelihood.

In this context, the Taliban has managed to present itself as a protector of local livelihoods by allowing opium production to continue in the areas under its control.

The depressing conclusion is that despite the vast injections of international capital flowing into the country and a universal desire to 'succeed' in Afghanistan, the state is once again in serious danger of falling into the hands of the Taliban. Where implemented, international development and reconstruction efforts have been underfunded, failed to have a significant impact on local communities' living conditions or improve attitudes towards the Afghan Government and the international community. The current insurgency, divided into a large poverty-driven 'grassroots' component and a concentrated group of hardcore militant Islamists, is gaining momentum, further complicating the reconstruction and development process and effectively sabotaging NATO-ISAF's stabilisation mission in the country.

Until the international community expands its focus beyond the traditional military dimensions, targeting needs at a grassroots level and thus restoring its previous levels of support, there is a danger that the Taliban will simply overrun Afghanistan under the noses of NATO.

Doubling the Troops to Bolster Development Efforts

Security must improve in parallel to development efforts. The Taliban will succeed for as long as they are fighting an under-resourced power. To demonstrate to the Afghan people that NATO is offering nothing short of an unwavering commitment to the fight, ISAF must have access to formidable military force. With some NATO members restricted by caveats, this is not the case.

The total number of international troops integrated to ISAF urgently needs to be doubled to a minimum of 80,000 troops. Currently, NATO is in command of the International

Force and most ISAF troops are provided by NATO member states. Nevertheless, contributions from individual countries are, even within NATO, largely uneven when considered in proportion to their population or GDP [gross domestic product]. For instance, France and Spain are contributing less than one soldier per billion USD [U.S. dollars] of GDP while the United Kingdom and Turkey each supply above three soldiers per USD billion.

Increasing troop levels alone is not sufficient to succeed. Security and development are two inseparable sides of the same reconstruction effort. Development without security and the rule of law would certainly lead to Afghanistan's disintegration. On the other hand, security at the expense of development is not sustainable; social and economic development is essential to long-term political stability. A lack of real governance and stability is creating a breeding ground for conflict, further instability and violence.

Improving the Lives of Afghans

The international community's strategy in Afghanistan must be a serious commitment to improve the lives of Afghans in an immediate and substantial manner. This is essential in counteracting the Taliban's propaganda against the West and the Afghan Government. A coherent hearts and minds strategy to address the poverty in Afghanistan's southern provinces will help international troops achieve their mission.

For the reconstruction effort to be an unambiguous success story, it is essential that the international community creates clearly defined goals in terms of development. Currently, Afghanistan is littered with challenges such as high maternal mortality rates, a failure to adequately promote secondary education, high unemployment and mass displacement due to drought, crop failure, forced opium eradication and destruction of villages during combat between international and insurgent forces.

These are areas that the West must focus on improving, setting priorities, sequencing and creating positive impact on the lives of the Afghan people. Multidimensional poverty represents a direct threat to the achievements of the Bonn process [the Bonn Agreement was the initial series of agreements intended to recreate the state of Afghanistan following the U.S. invasion]. Rising levels of violence and support of the Taliban show the need for the new democratic institutions to deliver meaningful, pro-poor, policies to the population. Poverty is the primary enemy of Afghanistan's reconstruction, and must be defeated. As a beneficiary of international aid, Afghanistan receives the lowest amount of reconstruction financing compared to all other post-conflict nations, signifying a failure to recognize that Afghanistan is among the poorest of the poor nations. The response to emergency crises like starvation is not only a humanitarian necessity—it represents an essential part of any stabilization effort.

The international community's policy in Afghanistan must be to bring about the conditions in which social and economic development can ultimately be created and sustained by the Afghans themselves. It is key that the international community does not allow the conflict to impact on the futures of the youth of Afghanistan. Improving literacy and education, providing healthcare, creating the necessary infrastructure, and providing economic choice through licit sources of revenue and job opportunities are all essential to Afghanistan becoming an economically robust state which is capable of democratic self-governance. An Afghan Community Fund, similar to Brazil's Bolsa Familia project, should be set up, whereby positive actions from the Afghan public would be rewarded with mutual investment on the part of the government supported by the international community.

Securing Afghanistan's stable and prosperous future requires a young generation of competent, peace-driven Afghans to take the leadership. Leadership training for the young unemployed and conflict-ravaged Afghans should be organised seeking to provide them with the necessary skills to assume leadership from current stakeholders, who are the victims of decades of conflict, civil strife and tribal tensions.

The international community has a crucial role to play in building local capacities and strengthening Afghan ownership, by forging connections between Afghans, by investing in infrastructure, healthcare and education, as well as investing in locally supported delivery systems. Afghan ownership of the development situation is a politic way forward as it helps build public confidence and trust in the Afghan Government and the international community.

CHAPTER 2

Can Democracy Work in Afghanistan?

Chapter Preface

Afghan politics were dramatically altered by the 2001 U.S. invasion of Afghanistan and the ejection of the Taliban government. With the assistance of the United Nations, an interim government was created that agreed on a new democratic constitution. On October 9, 2004, it was estimated that more than three-quarters of the country's nearly ten million registered voters went to the polls to vote in democratic presidential elections. Voters overwhelmingly supported Hamid Karzai, a former anti-Taliban fighter, as Afghanistan's president. Legislative elections were held the following year, on September 18, 2005, to fill positions in the country's legislature, the National Assembly. Both sets of elections were peaceful and successful despite threats of Taliban violence. Buoyed by these successes, the people of Afghanistan hoped that their country could finally move forward, both politically and economically.

According to most observers, however, Afghanistan's new democracy has became infected with corruption. Citizens complain that virtually every public service or administrative action requires a bribe. People who want to obtain a license to start a business, get electricity for their homes, or resolve a judicial dispute regarding title to property are routinely asked to pay hefty bribes for the privilege. People are even asked to pay for small things—to process paperwork, enter the airport, or drive to their destinations without being stopped or harassed. Money also can buy more important things, such as government jobs and releases from jail. In addition, the police reportedly demand bribes from drug-runners and other criminals to look the other way—a situation that dangerously undermines the country's system of law and order. And the corruption may exist even at the top levels of government, where some officials are suspected to be involved in embezzling funds from international aid sent to Afghanistan.

Various studies have documented the corruption problem in Afghanistan. In 2007, the international anti-corruption organization, Transparency International, ranked Afghanistan 172 out of the 179 countries surveyed on its corruption-perceptions index. That same year, a survey of Afghan citizens by the independent group, Integrity Watch Afghanistan, found that 60 percent of Afghans believe their current leaders are even more corrupt than the Soviet-backed government that ruled in the 1980s or the Taliban-run government of the 1990s. Even President Karzai has admitted that his government is mired in corruption.

Experts say much of the corruption in Afghanistan is fueled by the country's extreme poverty and inability to fund clean government. Low-paid government workers, therefore, use bribes to pad their salaries. And policemen and judges are not only low-paid but also untrained and surrounded by a culture of corruption. In the end, the weak law enforcement allows bribery and corruption to flourish without prosecution, completing the cycle of lawlessness. Other contributing factors to Afghanistan's corruption problem include widespread poppy cultivation that produces opium for illegal drug operations. Many farmers and rural poor Afghans rely on poppies to earn a living, and the illegal drug economy created by this industry depends on paying off police and government officials with bribes. In a poor country such as Afghanistan, drugs can bring fabulous wealth to those willing to take the risks.

Many people fear that government corruption is undermining the legitimacy of Afghanistan's democracy. If things do not improve, Afghans may support the return of the Taliban, who for all their excesses and brutality, some argue, at least brought law and order, security, and uniform justice to Afghanistan. Despite these dangers, President Karzai has so far been unable or unwilling to stamp out the corruption problem. Afghans have criticized Karzai's appointment of warlords and tribal leaders to government posts despite evidence that these officials might be corrupt, and some commentators have claimed that Karzai has willingly overlooked clear incidents of corruption among high-level government officials. Karzai also may be losing U.S. and international support; although Karzai won presidential elections held in August 2009, there were reports of widespread fraud which prompted a recount and may result in a wider investigation and ultimately in a runoff election. In addition to electing new leaders, commentators have suggested attacking the corruption problem by asking foreign governments to send civilian aid workers to Afghanistan, to help the country foster a better trained and less corrupt police force and civil service.

Other threats to Afghanistan's democracy include the long history of tribal divisions within the country's population, the lack of clear political parties, and the rising Taliban insurgency. Whether Afghanistan can overcome the many problems facing its democracy has yet to be decided. The viewpoints in this chapter debate the critical question of whether Afghanistan's democracy is likely to succeed.

The Afghan National Assembly Has the Potential to Bring Democracy to Afghanistan

International Crisis Group (ICG)

The International Crisis Group (ICG) is an independent, non-profit, multinational organization based in Brussels, Belgium, that works to prevent and resolve deadly conflict.

The new National Assembly has the potential to play a vital role in stabilising Afghanistan, entrenching pluralism, institutionalising political competition and giving voice to the country's diverse population. By being accountable to the Afghan people it can demand accountability of the presidential government. However, the success of this fledgling institution remains delicately poised, particularly because of the absence of a formal role for political parties, essential for mediating internal tensions. The lack of such organised blocs has seen power-brokers of past eras try to dominate proceedings. New moderate forces need to move quickly now to establish formal groups within the houses to ensure their voices are heard.

The Exclusion of Political Parties

The Single Non-Transferable Voting (SNTV) system used in the 2005 legislative election all but excluded political parties, which are vital for the development of robust democracy. [Afghan] President Hamid Karzai has done all he can to marginalise these parties, leaving him isolated and dependent on unstable alliances in a fragmented body. He probably can win votes of confidence by relying in the main on Pashtun conser-

International Crisis Group (ICG), *Afghanistan's New Legislature: Making Democracy Work. Asia Report, No. 116*, Washington, D.C.: International Crisis Group, 2006. Reproduced by permission.

vatives together with pro-government moderates and members of the smaller minority communities. However, the absence of solid political blocs means he will have to assemble ad hoc support on every issue. Ethnic politics has been, and indeed will likely remain, one of the main organising factors but would be better brought out into the open within formalised blocs.

The rules of procedure allow these as mechanisms—called parliamentary groups in the lower house, and political groups in the upper house—to facilitate efficient parliamentary operation. However, many impulses for their creation—regional, linguistic and tribal—are barred, rendering them all but meaningless. And even then the formation of such emasculated groups has been delayed in the lower house. If parties were required to have charters stipulating internal democratic functioning, their formation based on any criteria should be encouraged also as a means to stimulate the development of true political parties. Given that no one ethnic group has a majority in either house of the assembly, ongoing compromise would be demanded.

That the [Afghan] legislature contains warlords, commanders and drug traffickers is undisputed.

A Shaky Beginning

In its opening months, the bicameral legislature has functioned slowly but encouragingly steadily, emphasising procedural decision-making. Tedious discussion and repetitive voting on the same topics have hopefully demonstrated to lawmakers the importance of building more formal blocs to organise proceedings as well as the importance of following well-defined procedures.

There have been victories for the opposition, with a Karzai rival elected to head the more important Wolesi Jirga (lower house), though the government secured confirmation of major ministers in a key vote. Fears of deadlock through obstructionism, the sheer amount of work to get through and inexperience have translated into a tendency towards a lack of oversight and acceptance of governmental preferences. But as legislators gain confidence and experience, such acquiescence cannot be relied on. Building good relationships between the institutions of state needs to be a priority now.

That the legislature contains warlords, commanders and drug traffickers is undisputed, but it is the institution, not the individual members, that is important. Their presence must not be used as an excuse to marginalise the body, which in this sense is not unique among the branches of the Afghan state. A policy of co-option over the last four years has entrenched notorious figures in the executive, from the highest central government posts to district level. Those who have committed and are still committing atrocities—in many cases with remarkable continuity—are not held answerable, highlighting the urgent need to reform the third branch, the judiciary. Commitments to disarmament that many candidates made to qualify to stand for election must also be rigorously monitored.

The National Assembly could force religious and factional leaders, who have long claimed to speak for the Afghan people, to prove their real levels of support, which there is good reason to believe is in some cases far less than they assert. It is also a place in which the first stirrings of new national thinking may appear. Under a quota system, around one quarter of its membership is female, in noticeable contrast to the executive. As it moves into substantive work, the National Assembly has real potential to draw the regions to the centre in a way that has not happened in Afghanistan's history.

The Need for International Support

But for the legislature—and democratic values—to take root, domestic recognition and international support are required. This is not just about finances, resources and training, but also executive branch and international community interaction with it. National Assembly leaders as well as the emerging moderate voices need to be given appropriate recognition and encouragement. Thus far President Karzai's government does not seem to have learnt the lessons of the past, appearing instead to calculate that a weak, fragmented legislature would mean more power for itself rather than a lost opportunity for the country. It is imperative that the executive and legislative branches not approach their relationship as a zero sum game.

One of the primary tasks of elected representatives in a democracy is usually to mediate the allocation of resources. Afghanistan is in an unusual situation in that donors control nearly all its resources. Nevertheless, the international community can expect to find the National Assembly a demanding interlocutor. Amid growing disillusionment at the pace of political and economic reconstruction, this is the forum from which to start managing expectations and hearing the priorities of the Afghan people. It must also perform a vital role if the ambitious regulatory and legislative benchmarks laid down in the Afghanistan Compact as conditions for ongoing international commitments are to be met.

For the legislature—and democratic values—to take root [in Afghanistan], domestic recognition and international support are required.

It is also vital that Afghanistan have functioning institutions to implement the decisions of its democratic law-making body. If the National Assembly is not seen to be achieving anything, citizens are likely to lose faith in democratisation as a whole, allowing old powerbrokers to reassert themselves outside constitutional structures. The need to ensure implementation of laws highlights again how vital it is to reform and strengthen the civil service, police and other institutions of state.

The National Assembly's creation was just one further step in the country's political transition, certainly not its end. A well-established, accountable and respected legislature would add to stability by allowing a wide spectrum of voices to be heard at the centre and to participate in setting the country's future course. The considerable goodwill and energy that is at hand now needs to be harnessed.

Free and Fair Elections Could Improve Afghanistan's Democracy

Daoud Sultanzoy

Daoud Sultanzoy is an Afghan member of Parliament in Afghanistan's National Assembly (Wolesi Jirga). He also is chairman of Afghanistan's National Economy Committee.

Looking at Afghanistan, its democracy and its future, it is very clear many golden opportunities for improvement have been lost over the past seven years.

Lost, first and foremost, by the Afghan leadership for not being able to do its part in every single aspect of governance. But also lost by the international community for not fully recognizing the importance of a more transparent, disciplined, and coherent approach to tackling the problems in Afghanistan.

The international community now has to refocus on the reality they know. This reality includes the lowest life expectancy in the world. It includes poverty, poor health care and poor education. And it includes a shortage of other services despite the (albeit insufficient) aid and money poured into the country.

[Afghanistan's younger generation] are wondering what is going to happen to them in terms of daily living, jobs and simple aspects of life.

Worries About the Future

The people of Afghanistan know what the problems are: corruption, waste, lack of co-ordination, indecisiveness and prob-

Daoud Sultanzoy, "Afghanistan (Part 1): The Issues: Elections in Afghanistan—A Potential Tipping Point," *NATO Review*, Summer 2008. Reproduced by permission.

lems stemming from failed leadership, which has hindered aid delivery and reconstruction. They know that the reasons for problems have not changed, just the emphasis on discussing them. The future of Afghanistan depends on these people. They are aware that the international community's involvement is now a life or death factor for their nation.

There has been much discussion of issues like rule of law, good governance, justice and drugs. But other key aspects of rescuing Afghanistan have been neglected.

There are some issues that the people of the country, especially the younger generation (who comprise a dramatic 85% of the population), are worried about. Plainly put, they are wondering what is going to happen to them in terms of daily living, jobs and simple aspects of life. They are likewise concerned with the political future of their country, which is connected to their own, personal well-being.

They are asking basic questions like:

- How serious is a democracy if the generation of the future, the majority, indefinitely see themselves ruled by the old guards of the dark ages?

- What would the continuation of this mean for democracy and the perception of democracy in Afghanistan and beyond?

- Who is providing real and meaningful support to the democrats, while others of dubious credentials and anti-democratic forces have multiple sponsors and are set on undoing democratisation and harmony?

Citizens will be driven toward extremism and criminality, and . . . it will be increasingly difficult to restore control and order.

It is vital to realise that younger generations of Afghans are at a crossroads. They are watching as bystanders while others (who do not understand them) are making all the decisions for them. They do not feel part of the political process.

This is due to their lack of integration into meaningful social and political programmes, in addition to the Afghan leadership's inability to galvanise and lead. Similarly, this leadership does not address the immediate needs of its citizens, thereby creating a disconnect between the population and government.

And What Happens if Democracy Doesn't Work . . . ?

Here's the risk: this inadequate relationship is further driving people away from the mainstream, and creating opportunities for distrust in the authority that so vehemently stated it would fulfill its promises. Citizens will be driven toward extremism and criminality, and once these occurrences fully unravel, it will be increasingly difficult to restore control and order.

These issues are not only of major concern to the younger Afghan generation, but should also be immediately addressed by our allies and the Afghan government.

The approaching political season in the country should bring much-needed attention to these issues [of Afghanistan's needs].

The approaching political season in the country should bring much-needed attention to these issues. This especially significant political time can provide necessary awareness of Afghanistan, and that its people need much more than what the international community and Afghan government have been talking about.

Finding adequate responses to these needs could create the essential impetus and catalyst so the people can become part of the process—and not simply observe as bystanders.

No nation can be built if its people do not feel a sense of ownership.

No people can have a sense of ownership if they do not feel part of the process.

No process will succeed if it lacks proper leadership.

No leadership can lead if it is void of credibility.

The Importance of Free and Fair Elections

With these facts in mind we must examine:

- Whether there is a danger that non-democrats could hijack a new democracy in Afghanistan.

- The need to give Afghans a sense of ownership of this democracy.

- The need for Afghans to make the democratic process more accountable.

- The importance of the coming elections.

- The need to demonstrate a peaceful transfer of power from one leader to another.

Free and fair elections are at the heart of the issue. To show our seriousness as a group of nations in our promise to help Afghanistan, we must fully equip ourselves to fulfill our commitment.

Free and fair elections are at the heart of the issue.

Fair elections would allow the people of Afghanistan—for the first time in their modern history—to change leadership from one president to another elected president peacefully, affording people the much-needed sense of democratic ownership. This is immeasurably important for nation-building and democracy promotion.

Fair elections will provide a new flexibility and patience in people who have been largely frustrated and exhausted. Local ownership will allow the new leadership and international partners to learn from the past mistakes and resume a rein-vigorated reconstruction and reform process.

Fair elections will also re-engage and re-stimulate the con-stituencies of all countries involved in helping Afghanistan. It will tell them that the efforts of the past seven or eight years were not a waste—and the process is bearing fruits.

I see that the Afghan government has already begun to rig the elections through various tactics, right under the nose of the international community. If this misuse and abuse of power is tolerated, people will interpret this as a nod by the allies of Afghanistan. I believe that such abuse would derail any future chances of having the Afghan people on the side of international community.

Similarly, international community support for an admin-istration that rigs elections will be a blow to democracy and its own reputation.

The desires of the Afghan people are no different from other peoples or nations. Meaningful and long-lasting change is what the people want.

If we fail to recognise this much-needed aspiration, then a nation will arise whose majority will side with the opponents of democracy. Disillusionment will lead to widespread ex-tremism and criminality, and we may be left with a nation who will no longer trust any system of governance.

The ramifications of such failure and loss of credibility by the international community in Afghanistan will not be lim-ited just to Afghanistan. Its reverberations will be felt through-out the region, the entire Islamic world, and beyond.

The United States Is Committed to a Democratic Afghanistan

George W. Bush

George W. Bush was the 43rd president of the United States.

A fghanistan is a dramatically different country than it was eight years ago. When I took office in 2001, the Taliban [a fundamentalist Islamic militia] was brutally repressing the Afghan people. Girls were denied access to school. People who did not submit to the regime's radical beliefs were beaten in public, or executed in soccer stadiums. Al Qaeda [an international terrorist network led by Osama bin Laden] had free rein to operate the country—in the country. And it was here in Afghanistan that the terrorists planned the attacks of September 11th, 2001.

After that date, America gave the Taliban a choice: You can turn over the leaders of al Qaeda, or you can share in their fate. And when they refused, our just demands were enforced by the United States military. And thanks to you, the Taliban has gone from power, the al Qaeda training camps are closed, and 25 million Iraqis are free. And the American people, your loved ones, are more secure.

Democracy for Afghanistan

Removing the Taliban was a landmark achievement. But our work did not end there. See, we could have replaced one group of thugs with another strongman. But all that would have done is invited the same problems that brought us the al Qaeda safe havens and the attacks on America in the first place. Those were the mistakes of the 1980s and 1990s, and

George W. Bush, "President Bush Visits with Troops in Afghanistan," The White House, Office of the Press Secretary, December 15, 2008.

we were not going to repeat them again in the 21st century.

So America set an ambitious goal—to help Afghanistan's young democracy grow and thrive, and emerge as an alternative to the ideology of hate and extremism and terror. This is a difficult and long effort. It's not easy to do this. It would have been so much simpler to say we got rid of one bunch and here's another one. But that's not what we believe is right. We want to lay the foundation of peace for generations to come. We want to do the hard work now so our children and our grandchildren can grow up in a peaceful world.

Removing the Taliban was a landmark achievement.

So we rallied good allies to our side, including every member of NATO [North Atlantic Treaty Organization, an alliance of European and North American countries]. We've developed civilian experts in the form of civilian reconstruction teams. And together with the determined people of Afghanistan, we are making hopeful gains.

Thanks to you, girls are back in school across Afghanistan. Does that matter? I think it does. I think it does. Thanks to you, boys are playing soccer again, and flying kites, and learning to be Boy Scouts. Thanks to you, access to health care is up dramatically. Thanks to you, Afghanistan's economy has more than doubled in size. And thanks to you, the Afghan people are preparing to go to the polls next year [2009] for another round of free elections. Thanks to you, Afghanistan has a democratic government that is no longer an enemy of America; it is a friend of America.

The U.S. Commitment to Afghanistan's Democracy

The enemies of freedom in Afghanistan are determined, no question about it, and the fight has been tough—I don't need to tell you. This is a large country; it has a long way—it's a long way away from a modern economy with a viable infrastructure. It's hard to get around Afghanistan. Yet we have a strategic interest, and I believe a moral interest in a prosperous and peaceful democratic Afghanistan. And no matter how long it takes, we will help the people of Afghanistan succeed.

Afghanistan has a democratic government that is no longer an enemy of America; it is a friend of America.

As a sign of our commitment, we've increased American troop levels in Afghanistan. Our NATO allies have done the same. And so have the Afghan people—Afghan army and police have grown. I call it a quiet surge. It's a surge that hadn't gotten much attention. But it has an unmistakable message: The Taliban has gone from power, and it's not coming back. Al Qaeda terrorists have lost their safe haven in Afghanistan, and they're not going to get it back. Afghanistan will be a successful society and a hopeful society and a free society. And Afghanistan will never again be a safe haven for terrorists to attack the United States of America.

In recent months, the violence has increased in some parts of Afghanistan. This is partly because we're going into new areas where the terrorists have never been challenged before. And if the enemy are fighting back, they don't like it when we show up. But ultimately, they will be no match for the Afghan people or her coalition partners. And they're certainly no match for the men and women of the United States military.

I am confident we will succeed in Afghanistan because our cause is just, our coalition and Afghan partners are determined; and I am confident because I believe freedom is a gift of an Almighty to every man, woman, and child on the face of the Earth. Above all, I know the strength and character of you all. As I conclude this final trip, I have a message to you, and to all who serve our country: Thanks for making the noble choice to serve and protect your fellow Americans.

What you're doing in Afghanistan is important, it is courageous, and it is selfless. It's akin to what American troops did in places like Normandy and Iwo Jima and Korea. Your generation is every bit as great as any that has come before. And the work you do every day is shaping history for generations to come.

Because of you, America has a strong friend and partner in the fight against extremism in a pivotal part of the world. Because of you, people across the broader East—Middle East now have an example of a more hopeful path—a model of liberty that can prevail over tyranny and terror. Because of you, killers who wanted to take the lives of Americans back home have been brought to justice before they reached our shores. And because of you and all who work to protect our nation, America has done something many said was impossible: We have gone more than seven years without a terrorist attack on our homeland.

This time of year is especially a time when we thank the Almighty for our freedoms. And we think of those who laid down their lives to protect those freedoms. Back home their children are growing up without a mom or a dad. But all of our children are growing up with something else—the promise of a safer America, the promise of a better world, and the more likelihood for peace.

This is a lasting memorial—all who have sacrificed here in Afghanistan. And thanks to you, that memorial will be achieved, and the sacrifice of your comrades will not have been in vain. We think of the comrades who have been wounded. Our nation pledges that we will give them all the care and all the support they need to recover.

And finally, we think of your families back home. You've got a loved one wondering what you're doing, how you're doing—I want you to do me a favor: When you get back to wherever you're getting back to, call them, e-mail them, or write them. Tell them you love them, and tell them the

Commander-in-Chief thanks them for their sacrifice, thanks them for loving you like they do, and thanks for—thank them for standing with you as you serve the noble cause of peace.

I am proud to be with you. I thank you from the bottom of my heart. May God bless you, and may God continue to bless the United States of America.

Democracy in Afghanistan Is in Danger

International Federation for Human Rights

The International Federation for Human Rights is a federation of non-governmental human rights organizations.

The International Federation for Human Rights (FIDH) [a group of human rights organizations] expresses its concern regarding the regression of democracy in [Afghanistan] . . . and calls for the unconditional release of Latif Pedram, under house arrest since the 2nd of February 2008. . . .

Barring War Criminals from Afghanistan's Democracy

The next presidential elections will take place in 2009 and the parliamentary elections in 2010. The FIDH calls for the revision of the eligibility criteria in order to stop old war criminals or any person responsible for crimes against humanity from being candidates, and to promote democratic forces. This commitment had been made, under the previous parliamentary elections, to guarantee that no former war criminal or person responsible for crimes against humanity be eligible for parliamentary elections. Nonetheless, this commitment didn't have much effect and thus many former war criminals found themselves on the benches of the Afghan parliament, where they blocked numerous opportunities for democratic and institutional reforms.

The last two elections have been marred by serious irregularities. The international community must ensure that the Afghan authorities organise the fairest elections possible by organising a pre-electoral population census in order to redraw the electoral map, until now based on estimations. This census was supposed to start in July [2008]. On the 8th of June [2008], the Afghan Central Bureau of Statistics announced its postponement for two years, claiming a "politicisation" of the exercise, a somewhat strange response as it concerns the preparation of an exercise in political expression. . . .

Situation of Latif Pedram

Latif Pedram is an author, a renowned politician in Afghanistan and a staunch pacifist. He sought refuge in France during the Taliban [a fundamentalist Islamic militia] period between 1993 and 2004 as a fervent opponent to their policies; he mobilized international public opinion in favour of democracy and Human rights in his country.

He returned to Afghanistan in 2004 after having founded the National Congress of Afghanistan, a democratic and multi-ethnic political party for democratic change in Afghanistan, notably affiliated to the International Socialists and the European Socialist Party.

Last February 2nd [2008], Latif Pedram was placed de facto under house arrest, in a house surrounded by the police and security forces from the Ministry of Interior, by order of the Attorney General. The latter notably forbade him to leave the territory for having allegedly witnessed an altercation between two Afghani political personalities. Latif Pedram had merely been asked to facilitate the dialogue between these two politicians.

The International Federation for Human Rights (FIDH) considers that these accusations are unfounded and politically motivated in order to curtail his political activities and hinder his candidacy for next year's presidential elections.

The man responsible for his house arrest, Attorney General [Abdul Jabbar] Sabit, a former member of the Islamist

Party (Hezb-e-Islami), has indeed shown, on a number of occasions, his hostility towards progressive ideas and personalities.

Latif Pedram's house arrest created an unprecedented popular movement and thousands of people rushed to visit him. The house arrest occurs in a context wherein a number of pacifist and democratic personalities from civil society are deliberately being targeted (as in the case of the parliamentarian Malalay Joya), threatened with death (the President of the National Human Rights Commission Mrs Sima Samar), when they aren't assassinated (lately, the BBC correspondent Abdelsamad Ruhani.)

The FIDH would like the international community to mobilise itself and secure ... :

- Latif Pedram's release

- that the charges against him be dropped

- that his safety be guaranteed

- that he will be able to return fully into the political and democratic life of the country

---

The Afghani population ... are faced with a government that has failed to engage the necessary democratic reforms.

Upcoming Elections

2009 will see the next presidential elections in Afghanistan and 2010, the parliamentary elections. . . .

If the last elections were marred by serious irregularities, they nonetheless consecrated the rejection of the Taliban regime by the Afghan population. However, six years later, the frustration is great amidst the Afghani population who are faced with a government that has failed to engage the necessary democratic reforms. This frustration could translate itself into a shunning of the ballot box by a majority of the population, despite the Taliban menace over the elections that remain clear and present.

In this context, the international community must ensure that the Afghan authorities organise elections within maximum democratic conditions, so as to safeguard from all accusations of ballot rigging and to reinforce the space for democracy.

Three sets of recommendations need to be implemented:

- *Ensure legal and representative elections:*

  In order to do this, it is important to initiate a pre-electoral population census, so as to redefine the electoral map that is based on estimates rather than a proper demographic census. This exercise would also enable to clarify the situation of the populations living at the Pakistani border and avoid—as had been the case during the previous elections—Pakistani nationals voting in the Afghan elections.

  The Afghan authorities have so far refused to initiate this census, claiming the 'politicisation' of the exercise, a somewhat strange response as it concerns the preparation of an exercise in political expression.

- *Support the expression and representation of political parties:*

  Ruled out from the parliamentary election system (which is based on individuals and not on party lists), the political parties represent the necessary basis for the democratic debate that is lacking in Afghanistan. Nearly 80 political parties are officially registered in Afghanistan, some 15 of which are particularly active. The parties need to see their role enhanced and their public expression guaranteed in the independent media. Finally, they need to be represented in the Electoral Commissions that will be set in place for both elections.

- *Reinforce the criteria for eligibility:*

  During the previous elections, the transition government pledged that no war criminal or author of crimes against humanity would be eligible for the parliamentary elections. A sub-commission had been set-up within the Electoral Commission in order to receive, instruct and judge individual complaints against any candidate. Nonetheless, the majority of complaints received have not been enforced and thus many old war criminals found themselves on the benches of the Afghan parliament, where they blocked all opportunities for democratic and institutional reforms.

  For the next elections, it is essential to return to these criteria of eligibility and to guarantee their concrete implementation by the next Electoral Commission, with the support of the Independent Commission for Human Rights in Afghanistan.

Transitional Justice

After Hamid Karzaï's accession to power, there was a strong hope that the Afghan authorities would resolutely engage in the implementation of a mechanism for transitional justice, a tool for reconciliation and national peace and stability. This hope was further nourished by the signing of the Rome treaty on the International Criminal Court (ICC), the implementation of an independent National Commission for Human Rights and the adoption of an Action-plan for peace, justice and reconciliation.

Nonetheless, at the end of his mandate, the process for transitional justice is at a halt, as is shown by the adoption of the Amnesty law of March 2007 on the one hand, and the disappearance of demands relative to transitional justice from the conclusions of the international community addressed to Afghanistan on the other hand.

In a context where the rare voices in favour of credible mechanisms for truth and reconciliation are directly targeted or silenced (see the above-mentioned cases of Sima Samar, Latif Pedram and Malalay Joya), where the dialogue with the Taliban is taken up again without preconditions relative to the clarification of past crimes, it is essential to highlight the fundamental aspect of the fight against impunity, and to demand that the Afghan authorities follow their initial declarations with concrete and tangible actions.

The Dream of Democracy, Security, and Freedom Has Been Shattered

Revolutionary Association of the Women of Afghanistan (RAWA)

The Revolutionary Association of the Women of Afghanistan is a political/social organization of Afghan women working for peace, freedom, democracy and women's rights in Afghanistan.

Seven years back [2001] the US government and its allies were successfully able to legitimize their military invasion on Afghanistan and deceive the people of the US and the world under the banners of "liberating Afghan women", "democracy" and "war on terror". Our people, who had been tormented and oppressed by the Taliban's [a fundamentalist Islamic militia] dominance, were filled with hope but soon their dream of the establishment of security, democracy and freedom was shattered in the most painful manner.

The Failure of the Karzai Government

By the installation of the puppet government of [Afghan President Hamid] Karzai, the US reused its creations and continued its deal with the Jehadi criminal warlords. From the very start, Mr. Karzai shunned the demands and trusts of the people and chose to compromise with the criminals of the "Northern Alliance" [a group of Afghan tribal leaders] and placed the filthiest faces in the key posts of the government. In contradiction to the shameless claims of the ministers and other treacherous and corrupt officials, our people feel more ill-fated; the country has been turned to a mafia state and

Revolutionary Association of the Women of Afghanistan (RAWA), *Neither the U.S. nor Jehadies and Taliban, Long Live the Struggle of Independent and Democratic Forces of Afghanistan!* October 7, 2008. Reproduced by permission.

self-immolation, rape and abduction of women and children has no parallel in the history of Afghanistan.

Despite Karzai's pretence and crocodile tears, we witness that rapists are not only protected from persecution but forgiven, as Karzai announced amnesty for the people who had raped and then killed a woman and with this filthy act, soaked his hands in crime too!

On one hand, Karzai talks high of freedom of speech and democracy in his speeches and on the other hand a young journalist like Pervaiz Kambakhsh is behind bars and sentenced to death by the murderous band of Atta Mohammad; another brave journalist Naseer Fayyaz is forced to leave the country due to constant threats from big criminals including Ismail Khan and Qasim Fahim, and investigation by KHAD [Afghanistan's security agency] simply because he exposes the government and supports the truth. Some other noble and anti-fundamentalist people have been harassed and even harmed by the terrorists in power.

The people of the world should know that their aid is going to a government composed of fundamentalist criminals and technocrats . . . and their aid has no benefit for the common people of Afghanistan.

Karzai's government requested for $51 billion in the Paris Conference [an international conference in support of Afghanistan in 2008], [but when] . . . money flooded into Afghanistan [it] was not spent for the reconstruction of the country because of the atrocious corruption and indolence of ridiculous government officials. Moreover, people have been forced to sell their children due to destitution and starvation. The reality is that till now a big part of the aid have fattened the wallets and waists of the mafias of the "Northern Alliance", national and international NGOs [non-governmental organizations] and the corrupt governmental authorities. The people of the world should know that their aid is going to a government composed of fundamentalist criminals and technocrats who are also secret agents and corrupt to the marrow of bone and their aid has no benefit for the common people of Afghanistan.

The Failure of the War on Terror

The day to day expansion of the power of [the] Taliban reflects the real nature of the "war on terror" which has empowered the roots of fundamentalist terrorism more than ever. This is only a showcase to justify the long military presence of the US in our country and in the region. The result of this war has been such a huge failure that even political and military officials of the US and other countries have mentioned it very explicitly several times.

Instead of removing the cancerous lump of the Taliban and their Jehadi [holy war] brothers from the framework of Afghanistan, the troops of the US and its allies are bombarding wedding and joy parties and showering bullets on our oppressed people, especially women and children. Furthermore, when such crimes are exposed they shamelessly and haughtily deny them, and when the matter is proved, an arrogant "sorry" is offered, which pours more salt on the wounds of the people.

As we have declared many times, the US government has no and will not have any genuine concern for the condition of freedom, democracy and women's rights in Afghanistan. It is ready to accept a more corrupt, destructive and anti-democratic government than the one in power now, provided that its stooges are the rulers. Therefore today, some top criminals are being consistently freed from the prison. This clearly shows that "democracy" and "freedom of women" do not hold even an iota of value for the US administration and its allies in Afghanistan. They are planning to install a government made up of [Afghan] ... criminals; ... lackeys of the blood thirsty Iranian regime ...; and some other reactionary and treasonous elements related to the intelligence services of the West, so that even without direct military presence they would be able to control the country and save the country from becoming Iraq where the people rose against the US forces and its allies. If the US argues that it has not committed treachery, with the establishment of a government woven of the dirtiest enemies in the history of Afghanistan, they have committed the biggest possible treason against the Afghan nation, and they will not be able to justify this with any kinds of fabrications and cheatings. . . .

The troops of the US and its allies are bombarding wedding and joy parties and showering bullets on our oppressed people, especially women and children.

Afghanistan Must Fight for Its Own Freedom

RAWA [Revolutionary Association of the Women of Afghanistan] believes that in the present situation, elections will not give a better result than the previous one. In the conditions where all the governmental bodies are mainly under the reign of drug kingpin criminals and under the direct control of the US, most probably not even a handful of noble and independence-loving people will find [a] way into the parliament; therefore, the future parliament like today's will be home to the criminals and mafia whose life and status solely depend on dollars, weapons and the US support. If the US believes that Karzai has expired, it will bring another of its creation and won't allow an independent, democratic and antifundamentalist candidate to become the president with people voting freely.

The insignificance of our people's freedom desires and the actual aim of the US and its allies has reached to such an extent that a very bright example is when the Britain govern-

ment announces shamelessly that Afghanistan needs a dictator! Taking into account their contacts with the Taliban
terrorists, the most suitable dictator in their opinion must be
Mr. Mullah Omar. The US and its allies might control the
strings of the dirty puppet show in Afghanistan by their powerful war machines . . . , but they should be sure that this
treacherous spitting on democracy in Afghanistan and insult-
ing the will and anger of our people on ignorance, medieval
misogynists and Talibi and Jehadi fascism will be rubbed back
on their faces by our people.

It seems that if the invaders stop pretending and the dictator according to them should be Mullah Omar [a Taliban
leader] . . . then they should cancel or postpone the ridiculous
hard work of elections.

RAWA strongly believes that there should be no expectation of either the US or any other country to present us with
democracy, peace and prosperity. Our freedom is only achievable at the hands of our people. It is the duty of all the intellectuals, all the democratic forces and progressive and
independence-seeking people to rise in a constant and decisive
struggle for independence and democracy by taking the support of our wounded people as the independent force, against
the presence of the US and its allies and the domination of
Jehadi and Taliban criminals. Combating against the armed
and alien forces in the country without being loud-mouthed
against the Talibi and Jehadi enemies would mean welcoming
the misfortunes of fascism and religious mafia. Also, strug-
gling against this enemy without fighting the military presence
of the US, its allies and its puppet government would mean
falling before foreign agents. The path of the freedom-fighters
of our country without doubt, will be very complex, difficult
and bloody; but if our demand is to be freed from the chains
of the slavery of foreigners and their Talib and Jehadi lackeys,
we should not fear trial or death to become triumphant.

Warlordism Is Winning the Fight Against Democracy in Afghanistan

Radio Free Europe/Radio Liberty

Radio Free Europe/Radio Liberty is a news organization that broadcasts uncensored news and information in countries where a free press is either banned by the government or not fully established.

RFE/RL's [Radio Free Europe/Radio Liberty—a broadcasting company that promotes democracy by providing uncensored news to areas without a free press] Radio Free Afghanistan broadcaster Jan Alekozai spent [a month in Spring 2008] . . . in Kabul [Afghanistan's capital] and eastern Afghanistan, where he was often approached by students, local officials, and Afghan tribesmen who expressed their concerns about corruption, security, and distrust in the government. He spoke to RFE/RL correspondent Ron Synovitz about those concerns.

Ron Synovitz: During the past month when you were in Afghanistan, outside of your own efforts to speak with people from different segments of Afghan society, how were ordinary Afghans able to approach you and what were some of their concerns?

Jan Alekozai: I participated, for example, in a meeting [in Jalalabad]. It was the celebration of orange blossoms—a huge traditional gathering with 10,000 to 12,000 people. Someone announced my name—Jan Alekozai from Radio Free Afghanistan. When the meeting was over, hundreds of people approached me—students from high schools and from universities. They were asking, "Do the Westerners and the Americans know our problems—that aid money is coming from the Westerners but it goes into the pockets of [corrupt] people in the government offices."

That was their concern when they talked to me because they know I am running a call-in program on the airwaves of Radio Free Afghanistan. There were lots of concerns. They were desperately approaching me and asking those things—if we could bring their concerns to government officials. And they were expressing their concerns about their future and their lives, security, and education.

[Afghans] think now that [troops from] 37 countries or more are there in Afghanistan the security situations should be much, much better.

What did Afghans tell you bothered them most about the security situation in Afghanistan?

People think now that [troops from] 37 countries or more are there in Afghanistan the security should be much, much better. They should terminate the warlordism and the private militias. [Instead], those people have connections with the governmental officials and they still have protection from the government. And that brings insecurity. In Kabul, especially, but also elsewhere in other parts of the country.

People want the international community to stop the private militias—the groups that are so powerful. That's the main concern of the people, for security. And also, they should promote democracy. Real democracy. And work for that.

People are scared. They cannot say anything because of [the warlords]. We are an international radio [station]. We do something. But our correspondents, even, cannot say something against those warlords because they are very powerful. They could be killed easily or harmed easily. That's the situation. Everybody is asking why the international community doesn't hear.

Warlord Parliament

Who do Afghans think is responsible for the strengthening of warlords in Afghanistan today?

No. 1, the international community—or especially the Americans. They say: "Why have the Americans brought those people into power—the warlords? They knew they were warlords." And [Afghans] can name them for you—from the vice president to the deputy ministers and ministers. Quite a few were brought from outside.

In parliament, well-known warlords are there. In that situation, how do you expect [the] implementation of democracy and the rule of law—unless those people are removed from their positions and weakened, at least, and educated people are given a chance—[those] who think positively about the betterment of their country. Not for themselves. Those [warlords] are collecting money and putting the money in their pockets. They do little or nothing for the society and for the people.

[Warlords] are collecting money and putting the money in their pockets. They do little or nothing for the society and for the people.

How do Afghans think the warlords have been able to consolidate this power?

In parliament, 65 percent [of the lawmakers] are warlords. There is no question. A few of them are ordinary Afghans or politicians. But most of them are warlords. They are much stronger than they were six years ago or five years ago, because now they get more money, more security from the international community, more bodyguards. They get stronger and stronger.

Are there any specific examples of complaints from people about the increased power of warlords?

If you started from parliament or from the high governmental officials, you can see that warlordism is stronger than in years past. Television and other media cannot operate independently, if they do something and the next day they are in trouble in the parliament or with the high governmental officials.

In parliament, 65 percent [of the lawmakers] are warlords.

Foreigners Must Deal with Warlords

So if there is a conflict in Afghanistan now between warlordism versus democracy, which is winning?

At present, the warlordism is winning. If the international community does not pay attention—strongly—not by words. By action. They should eliminate the warlords. [The international community] thinks some of them are very strong. But they don't have public support.

I'm stressing this point. They are not that strong. They don't have public support because always they were thinking about themselves, their own pockets. They invest money outside of the country. People say that the Westerners, or in some ways they say the Americans, support these warlords. Otherwise they are nothing. They [say the warlords] were not powerful but [the Americans] made them powerful. And that was a main concern [of the Afghans].

It's very easy to remove them and bring in some people who have no connection with the warlords. And that would be real democracy that the people would enjoy.

Does this disdain for warlords contribute to feelings of anti-Americanism or to negative views about the international community?

I never heard people saying that they don't want Americans or international forces in their land. That was interesting for me. Even mullahs—the clerics I talked with and tribes-men. There were just a few who—like Taliban or pro-Taliban people—who said, "Oh, they are infidels."

But the majority of people, they never talked about that issue—why [foreign troops] are here. [Ordinary Afghans] think there is some propaganda from other neighboring coun-tries saying, "They are occupying your country." But to be honest, I haven't heard that from [ordinary Afghans]. They say, "Those people are here to help us." The only problem is that they don't trust the [Afghan] government. They also think that money is coming [to Afghanistan] from the inter-national community and from the Americans. But it goes into the wrong hands and into the wrong pockets.

[The warlords] are not that strong. They don't have pub-lic support because always they were thinking about themselves, their own pockets.

New Schools, Old Thinking

What about the reconstruction work being done by international nongovernmental organizations (NGOs) or by foreign troops on the provincial reconstruction teams, the so-called PRTs?

People say their general feeling is that they think the PRTs are doing well. They trust them because they say they are for-eigners and they are not corrupt—so far. But they don't like NGOs and there is no question that they don't trust the Af-ghan government at all. Still, people hope the PRTs will be doing well and probably will do something about road con-struction, about schools and other things. People count on PRTs.

U.S. officials often talk about the schools that have been built by PRTs as a positive step in the reconstruction of Afghanistan. Is this enough?

I've seen many schools that have been built and that are being built right now in different parts of eastern Afghanistan.

There's no doubt about it. Nice schools. But there is no teacher. No chairs—students are sitting on the floor. No electricity. No running water. No books. No [teaching materials]. No lab. What will be the quality of education in that situation?

The Talibanization or fundamentalist ideas are still very, very strong.

International media also report about greater rights and freedom for Afghan women since the collapse of the Taliban regime. How did that situation appear to you in the provincial regions as opposed to Kabul?

About the civil society or civic society, the participation of women is zero in the provinces. Girls are going to school. There is no doubt about it. But they cannot walk, for example, in a park—or even with their families.

Still the work is not done for the promotion of democracy and freedom. I think the culture is the same, with little changes in the mentality of the society. It is very bad. And it will continue like that now six years after the Taliban. The mentality is still very strong. The Talibanization or fundamentalist ideas are still very, very strong.

Presidential Challenger

All of these insights from ordinary Afghans suggests that Afghan President Hamid Karzai's popularity has declined dramatically since he was elected in 2004. Does Karzai have a chance to win reelection in the ballot that is scheduled for 2009?

As a journalist, one should talk with various people or people [with different political perspectives.] I learned [from doing this that something like] 25 percent or 20 percent will vote for Karzai. And I have doubts about [whether Karzai will even win that much of the vote.] It will be very difficult for him to get 20 percent. They need an alternative or another government.

Are ordinary Afghans talking about any potential candidate who they think would help reign in the power of warlords?

In the eastern part of Afghanistan—even in Kabul—people were talking [about this] when I was sitting with them. They said [former Interior Minister] Ali Ahmad Jalali. His name was being mentioned by people now. [They were saying] he is coming and he is a stronger man and he can do something. He can eliminate warlordism. They were talking about him, saying that if he is [a candidate] that people will vote for him and he will be the winner. That was the expectation of some when I talked to them.

Afghanistan Is High on Opium, Not Democracy

Robert Scheer

Robert Scheer is an American journalist and editor of Truth Dig, *a progressive online journal of news and opinion.*

The good news, for drug fiends, is that Afghanistan [in 2006] . . . harvested its biggest opium crop ever, up a whopping 59% from [2005] and big enough to cover 130% of the entire world market. The street price for illegal heroin, 92% of which now comes from Afghanistan, should be way down from Bangkok to London, and for those shooting up in the back alleys of Chicago. The bad news, for the rest of us, is that in [George W.] Bush-liberated Afghanistan, billions in drug profits are financing the Taliban [a fundamentalist Islamic militia].

Remember them, the guys who harbored the Al Qaeda [an international terrorist network led by Osama bin Laden] terrorists, who gifted us with the 9/11 attacks five years ago [in 2001], that President Bush promised to eliminate? Well, it turns out that while he was distracted with Iraq, the patrons of terrorism were very much in business back where the 9/11 attack was hatched, turning Afghanistan into a narco-state that provides a lucrative source of cash for the "evildoers" Bush forgot about.

The Bush administration has, for half a decade, celebrated its overthrow of the Taliban and subsequent national elections in Afghanistan, but if this is democratic nation-building then the model must be Colombia, the narco-state where the political process masks the real power held by drug lords and radical insurgents. Afghanistan is dominated not by the government in Kabul [Afghanistan's capital] but by a patchwork of warlords, terrorist groups and drug traffickers completely addicted to the annual poppy harvest's profits.

Or perhaps the model is post-invasion Iraq, because Afghanistan is now statistically as deadly for American soldiers, according to *The New York Times*, while in both countries suicide bombings and roadside bombings are on the rise and women are retreating to the burka to avoid persecution by armed zealots. In any case, reported the United Nations this week [in 2006], "opium cultivation in Afghanistan is out of control" despite the expenditure of billions by the West to fight it. Intelligence estimates of the Taliban's cut of this lucrative trade, which represents over a third of the entire Afghan economy, range up to 70%, according to *ABC News*.

"The political, military and economic investments by coalition countries are not having much visible impact on drug cultivation," reported the United Nations Office on Drugs and Crime in its authoritative annual survey. "As a result, Afghan opium is fueling insurgency in Western Asia, feeding international mafias and causing 100,000 deaths from overdoses every year." "The southern part of Afghanistan [is] displaying the ominous hallmarks of incipient collapse, with large-scale drug cultivation and trafficking, insurgency and terrorism, crime and corruption," added Antonio Maria Costa, the agency's director.

Afghanistan is dominated not by the government ... but by a patchwork of warlords, terrorist groups and drug traffickers ... addicted to the annual poppy harvest's profits.

Yet [in September 2006] ..., the White House was once again trumpeting that "we have deprived Al Qaeda of safe haven in Afghanistan and helped a democratic government rise in its place." Considering that Osama bin Laden himself is still reputed to be hiding somewhere along the Afghanistan-Pakistan border and Afghan President Hamid Karzai is desperately dependent on the support of drug lords and warlords to prevent renewed civil war, such claims are a blatant fraud. The senior British military commander in Afghanistan recently described the situation in the country as "close to anarchy" and said NATO [North Atlantic Treaty Organization, an alliance of European and North American countries] forces were "running out of time" to salvage the situation. "The narcotics industry accounts for over one-third of Afghanistan's gross domestic product and poses a threat to that country's stability and emerging democracy," carefully admits a recent U.S. State Department fact sheet.

What the Bush administration [did] . . . not confront in Afghanistan, or in Iraq, is that its ill-conceived and disastrously executed nation-building schemes are sinking into the swamp of local and historical realities. Enamored of American military might but having little understanding of the world beyond, Bush and his team have ignored [former Secretary of State] Gen. Colin Powell's reported "you break it, you own it" warnings, floundering after initial military victories and ultimately strengthening the hand of local and international terrorists. Rather than take care of business in Afghanistan after 9/11, Bush and clueless [former] U.S. Defense Secretary Donald Rumsfeld allowed bin Laden to slip out of the Tora Bora caves to plan more attacks and the Taliban to regroup. Instead, Bush and Co. threw the bulk of our military and aid resources into a disastrous attempt to remake oil-rich Iraq, which had nothing to do with 9/11, into an American puppet state. . . .

Embattled Republicans are now desperately claiming to be the only thing standing between us and a bogeyman they are calling "Islamo-fascism," and ridiculously comparing the "war on terror" to the fight against the Nazis. Fortunately, if belatedly, two-thirds of the American electorate now recognize that [former president Bush was] all hat and no cattle, as they say in Texas, a leader much better at starting wars than winning them.

CHAPTER 3

Should the U.S. Military Effort in Afghanistan Continue?

Chapter Preface

The war in Afghanistan escalated in 2008 and early 2009, as Taliban insurgents increased their attacks on U.S. and other NATO (North Atlantic Treaty Organization) coalition forces in the country. In fact, in 2008, insurgent attacks increased by 28 percent compared with the previous year. As a result, coalition deaths in the country also rose, ultimately outnumbering U.S. soldier deaths in Iraq that year. According to U.S. officials and other published reports, a total of 294 NATO soldiers were killed in Afghanistan in 2008, among them 155 Americans.

The number of troop deaths, however, pales when compared to the number of Afghan civilians killed in the fighting. According to a September 2008 report by the United Nations Assistance Mission in Afghanistan (UNAMA), 1,445 Afghan citizens were killed just in the first eight months of 2008—a 39 percent increase compared with the same period in 2007. Some civilians are caught in the gunfights between insurgents and NATO forces, while others are inadvertently hit in Taliban suicide attacks meant for Western troops. Increasingly, however, many civilians are victims of massive U.S. airstrikes. This growing problem of civilian deaths, often called collateral damage by military officials, is causing a backlash of outrage among the Afghan people and is fast becoming one of the most difficult problems for U.S. forces in the region.

U.S. military commanders explain that more civilians are being lost both because Taliban insurgents are paying Afghan civilians to fight Western forces and because insurgents are attacking from within villages and populated areas, essentially using civilians as human shields. As a result, U.S. soldiers have difficulty judging who the enemy is. Increasing support for the Taliban insurgency by local Afghans also has military leaders worried. Coalition forces have tried to limit civilian casualties and have sought to win the support of Afghan villagers by initiating reconstruction and development projects that offer good jobs. Yet according to reports from those on the ground, many young Afghan men appear to find it more exciting to earn the same amount of money working as paid fighters for the Taliban.

One of the most deadly and controversial incidents of civilian deaths occurred when U.S. airstrikes hit the village of Azizabad in August 2008. An inquiry conducted by the U.S. military concluded that the airstrike had killed 30 to 35 Taliban fighters but no more than seven villagers. Later, however, separate investigations by the United Nations, the Afghan government, and the Afghan Human Rights Commission found that 78 to 92 civilians had been killed, most of them women and children. Because of the discrepancy between the military and civilian reports, the United States announced it would conduct a new investigation to be led by U.S. Brigadier General Michael W. Callan. The Callan report, released October 1, 2008, concluded that 33 civilians had died in the strike, and rejected the methodology followed in investigations by the United Nations and others. The U.S. position was that the attack was necessary and that civilians died because they were being used as human shields by Taliban insurgents. The Callan report dismayed many observers who hoped it would be more conciliatory in tone and substance. Human Rights Watch, an international human rights organization, protested the report in a letter to U.S. Secretary of Defense Robert M. Gates, demanding that the United States take steps to reduce civilian casualties during military operations in Afghanistan. Other human rights advocates also have condemned the rising numbers of civilian casualties and the unrelenting U.S. air raids.

Afghanistan's President Hamid Karzai, too, has criticized the U.S. reliance on airstrikes and the carnage they cause for Afghan civilians. Following another U.S. airstrike on the village of Shah Wali Kot on October 3, 2008, for example, in which 40 civilians were killed and 28 wounded, Karzai publicly complained to U.S. officials. The October attack, according to witnesses, hit a wedding party as it traveled through the Kandahar region in southern Afghanistan, a region believed to be a Taliban stronghold. Karzai called on incoming President Barack Obama to end U.S. airstrikes that risk civilian casualties.

Commentators have warned that the rising numbers of civilian victims are angering the Afghan people and may obstruct the U.S. and NATO military operations in Afghanistan. The lack of accountability for civilian deaths and the absence of redress for both human life and property damage caused by American bombs, they say, could cause villagers to see the United States as their enemy rather than their protector. In fact, many observers fear that air raids and similar tactics that risk civilian lives, in the end, could turn the conflict into a battle by Afghans to remove foreign forces, rather than a war to save Afghanistan from the Taliban and other insurgents. Such a change in perception, many observers warn, would undermine U.S. interests in stabilizing the region and make the war much more difficult to win. The viewpoints in this chapter discuss the problem of civilian casualties and other obstacles to the U.S. effort to bring security to Afghanistan, and reveal some of the differing views about whether the operations are likely to succeed.

The War in Afghanistan Is a Necessary Part of the War on Terror

David Aaronovitch

David Aaronovitch is a writer and broadcaster on international politics and the media, and a columnist for The Times, *a British newspaper.*

Unsurprisingly, it has become common to hear the mournless rites being read for liberal interventionism. If anyone has opined publicly about Afghanistan in the last week [February 2008]—and plenty did—it was to regret our presence there and to wish us away. If ever an argument was being won by default this was it, especially since those making the case for quitting were far too exuberant to want to slow up and allow for the possible objections to their reasoning.

Rising Pessimism About Afghanistan

It was [U.S. Secretary of State] Condoleezza Rice, agitating for more NATO [North Atlantic Treaty Organization, an alliance of European and North American countries] troops to be deployed in Afghanistan, who precipitated the current poison-ivy rash of isolationist critiques. This week in Lithuania NATO defence ministers are meeting to discuss finding 7,500 more troops to reinforce the existing 42,000, and last week there was a run-in between the Americans and the Germans over whether Bundeswehr [Germany's armed forces] resources could be sent to the dangerous south—a spat that the Bundesmedia [German media] seemed to enjoy a bit too much.

To which many resonant voices here were raised to make this point: we don't have the men, and even if we did we

David Aaronovitch, "No Retreat from the War on Terror: If the West Backs Out of Afghanistan the Consequences Would Be Plainly Catastrophic," *The Times*, February 5, 2008. Copyright © 2008 Times Newspapers Ltd. Reproduced by permission.

shouldn't send them; in fact we should start talking about withdrawing the ones we've got because the whole thing is broken and cannot be mended. "We British," wrote Matthew Parris on Saturday on these pages [in *The Times*], "are at our limit and losing confidence in our usefulness." Independent reports speak of a danger of failure and a "weakening international resolve", and the few gains of our continued presence—"a few new schools and roads in the north", according to Simon Jenkins in *The Sunday Times*—are insufficient to stop the country fragmenting.

And it is worse than that, they imply, because most of the problems that exist we have ourselves provoked and indeed spread to neighbouring Pakistan. "To have set one of the world's most ancient and ferocious people [the [ethnic] Pashtuns] on the warpath against both Kabul [Afghanistan's capital] and Islamabad [Pakistan's capital] takes some doing. But Western diplomacy has done it," says Jenkins; though why the Pashtuns are any more ancient than the rest of us, and why it should be so surprising that "one of the world's most ferocious peoples" might be relatively easily provoked, he doesn't explain. The tribal areas of Pakistan and Afghanistan, he argues, should have been left alone.

Canada has already threatened to pull out its troops from [Afghanistan's] Kandahar province . . . if other NATO countries don't contribute more.

There has, of course, to be another logical step taken here, and this is it: for what cause have these bloody errors been committed? The cause of combating terror. But terror is an overblown threat, they say, exaggerated by men like [U.S. president George W.] Bush and [Pakistani president Pervez] Musharraf: terror kills few in the West and is generally contained by good policing. Our troops are making things worse.

Rather than a War on Terror, we might do better to talk of a musing on terror, or—at worst—the tiff with terror.

In the current circumstances of the failure of the opium strategy, the bloody fighting in Helmand [a province in Afghanistan], the row inside NATO and the argument about [British diplomat] Paddy Ashdown's unacceptability to Hamid Karzai, the Afghan President, [for the position of United Nations representative to Afghanistan] much of this pessimism seems appropriate. But if we are to follow its dictates, its proponents should do a better job of spelling out what it means. Anyone who still favours a military presence is easily decorated with the order of the armchair commentator, but let us see what other commentators are prepared to sit through.

Consequences of Pulling Troops Out of Afghanistan

Canada has already threatened to pull out its troops from Kandahar province in a year's time if other NATO countries don't contribute more. We must assume that if Britain were to begin to talk about a draw-down, then Canada would carry out this threat. British forces would then be exposed in Helmand and, presumably, would also withdraw. Let us suppose that an angry and abandoned US follows the "lead" offered by its allies, and itself pulls out, leaving itself only an air-to-ground interdiction capability.

Here are the likely consequences of such a pattern. The Afghan Government would collapse, to be replaced by an overt civil war fought between the Taleban [a fundamentalist Islamic militia] and local governors in the various provinces. A million or more Afghan refugees would again flee their country, many of them ending up in the West. Deprived of support from the US, as recommended by our commentators, President Musharraf or a successor would effectively withdraw from the border regions, leaving a vast lawless area from central Afghanistan to north central Pakistan. Al-Qaeda [an international terrorist network] and other jihadists would operate from these areas as they did before 9/11 [2001]. This time these forces—already capable of assassinating a popular democratic politician—would seriously impact upon the stability of Pakistan, which is a nuclear state.

Jihadists everywhere, from Indonesia to Palestine, would see this as a huge victory, democrats and moderates as a catastrophic defeat. There would hardly be a country, from Morocco to Malaysia, that wouldn't feel the impact of the reverse. That's before we calculate the cost to women and girls of no longer being educated or allowed medical treatment. And would there be less terror as a result?

We have been here before. After the Afghans managed to defeat the Russians, the Yanks—and everyone else—left Afghanistan alone, to be swallowed up by the Taleban. Who then let Osama bin Laden [leader of al Qaeda] in. It wasn't us who provoked the ferocious Pashtun [an Afghan ethnic sect] in 2001, it was their Mullah Omar [a Taliban leader] who gave sanctuary to the topplers of the twin towers. Many of bin Laden's people had themselves been radicalised by the failure of the West—in another non-intervention—to prevent Serb atrocities against Bosnian Muslims.

Jihadists everywhere, from Indonesia to Palestine, would see this as a huge victory, democrats and moderates as a catastrophic defeat.

Whatever the failures of Western policy—which have usually been about doing too little, not too much—they will not be dealt with by the creation of a new myth of non-interdependence. Just as the genocide in Darfur has refused to confine itself within the borders of the Sudan, but has now destabilised neighbouring Chad, so anything that happens in Pakistan or Afghanistan, whether we cause it or not, will come back to us in the shape of fleeing people, apocalyptic ideologues, weapons proliferation and the export of terror.

Fortunately, it isn't just [British Secretary of State] David Miliband who recognises this. . . . [U.S. president] Barack Obama [also recognizes] . . . that America must continue to be the ideological and physical arsenal of democracy. Thank God.

The United States Must Confront the New Crisis in Southern Afghanistan to Win the War on Terror

Barack Obama

Barack Obama, the Democratic candidate in the November 2008 U.S. presidential elections, was elected the 44th president of the United States.

[T]oday, October 22, 2008, I] just finished a meeting with Senator [Joe] Biden and members of my senior working group on national security. We had a wide-ranging discussion on the challenges facing our nation.

I've been pleased to draw on the support of these distinguished Americans during this [presidential] campaign. I was also honored to receive the support of [former U.S. Secretary of State] Colin Powell ..., who is a friend and former colleague to many of those here with me. General Powell is one of the finest soldiers and statesmen of our time. He has been a source of advice, and I look forward to drawing on his counsel—and the counsel of all of those standing with me today. . . .

Time for Fundamental Change

The next president will take office at a time of great uncertainty for America. We are in the midst of the greatest economic crisis since the Great Depression. And as challenging as our current economic crisis is, the next president will have to focus on national security challenges on many fronts. The terrorists who attacked us on 9/11 [2001] are still at large and

Barack Obama, "Obama's Statement on National Security," in *Real Clear Politics*, October 22, 2008.

plotting, and we must be vigilant in preventing future attacks. We are fighting two wars abroad. We are facing a range of 21st century threats—from terrorism to nuclear proliferation to our dependence on foreign oil—which have grown more daunting because of the failed policies of the last eight years.

To succeed, we need leadership that understands the connection between our economy and our strength in the world. We often hear about two debates—one on national security and one on the economy—but that is a false distinction. We can't afford another president who ignores the fundamentals of our economy while running up record deficits to fight a war without end in Iraq.

We must be strong at home to be strong abroad—that is the lesson of our history. Our economy supports our military power, it increases our diplomatic leverage, and it is a foundation of America's leadership and in the world. Through World War II, American workers built an Arsenal of Democracy that helped our heroic troops face down fascism. Through the Cold War [a period of tension between the United States and the Soviet Union], the engine of the American economy helped power our triumph over Communism.

The terrorists who attacked us on 9/11 are still at large and plotting, and we must be vigilant in preventing future attacks.

Now, we must renew American competitiveness to support our security and global leadership. That means creating millions of jobs in a new American energy sector, so that we're not borrowing billions from China to buy oil from Saudi Arabia—for the sake of our economy and our security, we must end our dependence on foreign oil. Keeping America ahead also calls for investments in American education, innovation and infrastructure, so that our kids can compete, our homeland is secure, and our country remains on the cutting edge.

It also means leading an international response to the financial crisis. On September 19th [2008], I called for a globally coordinated effort with our partners in the G-20 [a group of the world's most developed nations] to stabilize the credit markets. I'm happy that today, the White House announced a summit of the G-20 countries that provides an opportunity to advance the kind of cooperation that I called for last month. America must lead, and other nations must be part of the solution too.

We must recognize that from global economic turmoil to global terrorism, the challenges we face demand American leadership of strong alliances. When America is isolated, we shoulder these burdens alone, and the security and prosperity of the American people is put at risk. Yet for eight years, we have seen our alliances weakened and our standing in the world set back.

We cannot afford four more years of policies that have failed to adjust to our new century. We're not going to defeat a terrorist network that operates in eighty countries through an occupation of Iraq. We're not going to deny the nuclear ambitions of Iran by refusing to pursue direct diplomacy alongside our allies. We're not going to secure the American people and promote American values with empty bluster. It's time for a fundamental change, and that's why I'm running for president.

Ending the war [in Iraq] will help us deal with Afghanistan.

A New Direction in Afghanistan

This change must start with a responsible end to the war in Iraq. We shouldn't keep spending $10 billion a month in Iraq while the Iraqis sit on a huge surplus. Today, we discussed how to succeed in Iraq by transitioning to Iraqi responsibility.

For the sake of our economy, our military, and the long-term stability of Iraq, it's time for the Iraqis to step up.

Ending the war will help us deal with Afghanistan, which we talked about at length this morning. In 2002, I said we should focus on finishing the fight against Osama bin Laden [leader of al Qaeda who orchestrated the terrorist attacks of September 11, 2001]. Throughout this campaign, I have argued that we need more troops and more resources to win the war in Afghanistan, and to confront the growing threat from al Qaeda along the Pakistani border.

Over seven years after 9/11, the situation in Afghanistan is grave. This is the most violent year of the war, with the highest number of American casualties. The Taliban [a fundamentalist Islamic militia] is on the offensive, al Qaeda has a sanctuary across the border in Pakistan, and some experts believe that 50 percent of the Afghan economy comes from the heroin trade. As the Chairman of the Joint Chiefs of Staff recently said, "The trends across the board are not going in the right direction."

The Taliban is on the offensive, al Qaeda has a sanctuary across the border in Pakistan, and . . . 50 percent of the Afghan economy comes from the heroin trade.

Make no mistake: we are confronting an urgent crisis in Afghanistan, and we have to act. It's time to heed the call from General [David] McKiernan and others for more troops. That's why I'd send at least two or three additional combat brigades to Afghanistan. We also need more training for Afghan Security forces, more non-military assistance to help Afghans develop alternatives to poppy farming, more safeguards to prevent corruption, and a new effort to crack down on cross-border terrorism. Only a comprehensive strategy that prioritizes Afghanistan and the fight against al Qaeda will succeed, and that's the change I'll bring to the White House.

There is a clear choice in this election. On issue after issue, Senator [John] McCain has supported the key decisions and core approach of President [George W.] Bush. As president, he would continue the policies that have put our economy into crisis and endangered our national security. And as he's shown over the last few weeks, he would also continue the divisive politics that undercuts the bipartisan cooperation and national unity that is so badly needed in challenging times.

We need to change course. At home, we must invest in the competitiveness of the American economy. Abroad, we need a new direction that ends the war in Iraq, focuses on the fight against al Qaeda and the Taliban, and restores strong alliances and tough American diplomacy. To keep our country safe and prosperous, we need leadership that brings the American people together. That is the lesson of our history. Together, we cannot fail; together, we can rise to meet any challenge.

A U.S. Military Surge in Afghanistan Will Change the Dynamics in Afghanistan for the Better

Jason Straziuso and Rahim Faiez

Jason Straziuso and Rahim Faiez are writers for The Associated Press, *a worldwide news gathering organization.*

Kandahar Afghanistan—Afghanistan's southern rim, the Taliban's [a fundamentalist Islamic militia] spiritual birthplace and the country's most violent region, has for the past two years been the domain of British, Canadian and Dutch soldiers.

That's about to change.

U.S. Military Surge

In what amounts to an Afghan version of the surge in Iraq, the U.S. is preparing [in 2009] to pour at least 20,000 extra troops into the south, augmenting 12,500 NATO [North Atlantic Treaty Organization, an alliance of European and North American countries] soldiers who have proved too few to cope with a Taliban insurgency that is fiercer than NATO leaders expected.

New construction at Kandahar Air Field foreshadows the upcoming infusion of American power. Runways and housing are being built, along with two new U.S. outposts in Taliban-held regions of Kandahar province.

And in the past month the south has been the focus of visiting U.S. and other dignitaries—Sen. John McCain, Defense Secretary Robert Gates, U.S. congressional delegations and leaders from NATO headquarters in Europe.

Jason Straziuso and Rahim Faiez, "U.S. Readying Surge Against Taliban in Southern Afghanistan," *The Huffington Post*, January 1, 2009. Reproduced by permission.

For the first time since NATO took over the country in 2006, an experienced U.S. general, Brig. Gen. John Nicholson, is assigned to the south.

He says U.S. Gen. David McKiernan, NATO's commander in Afghanistan, has made the objectives clear in calling the situation in the south a stalemate and asking for more troops, on top of the 32,000 Americans already in Afghanistan.

Military officials say they have enough troops to win battles but not to hold territory, and they hope the influx of troops . . . will change that.

"By introducing more U.S. capability in here we have the potential to change the game," Nicholson said.

The Army Corps of Engineers will spend up to $1.3 billion in new construction for troop placements in southern Afghanistan, said the corps commander in Afghanistan, Col. Thomas O'Donovan.

Violence in Afghanistan has spiked in the last two years, and Taliban militants now control wide swaths of countryside. Military officials say they have enough troops to win battles but not to hold territory, and they hope the influx of troops, plus the continued growth of the Afghan army, will change that.

U.S. officials hope to add at least three new brigades of ground forces in the southern region, along with assets from an aviation brigade, surveillance and intelligence forces, engineers, military police and Special Forces. In addition, a separate brigade of new troops is deploying to two provinces surrounding Kabul [Afghanistan's capital].

Adm. Mike Mullen, chairman of the Joint Chiefs of Staff, said last month [December 2008] that Afghanistan could get up to 30,000 new U.S. troops in 2009, depending on the security situation in Iraq. Col. Greg Julian, a U.S. military spokesman, said . . . that one ground brigade should arrive by spring, a second by summer and a third by fall.

Nicholson said he expects the U.S. forces to be deployed in Kandahar city and along vital Highway 1, which links Kandahar to Kabul, and in neighboring Helmand province, the world's largest producer of opium poppies for heroin.

NATO forces are well positioned in three key areas of northern Helmand, said British Lt. Gen. J.B. Dutton, deputy commander of the NATO's Afghan mission.

"What we have not yet achieved is to join those areas up, so there is a security presence that allows locals to drive safely between those areas. That's the sort of thing we are going to want to improve," he said.

The infusion of U.S. power risks Americanizing a war that until now has been a shared mission of 41 coalition countries.

Since 2006, the U.S. has concentrated its forces in eastern Afghanistan, along the border with Pakistan, while the south is policed by 8,500 British troops, 2,500 Canadians and 2,500 Dutch.

Their overall commander is Dutch Maj. Gen. Mart de Kruif—who would also have command of any incoming U.S. forces in the south next year. By the fall of 2010 the top officer in the south will be American.

Intensified Fighting

The infusion of U.S. power risks Americanizing a war that until now has been a shared mission of 41 coalition countries. But Dutton, the British general, suggested there was no choice. "It has to do with national capacity and a number of political considerations in those countries," he said.

In Canada and many European countries, governments face low public support for keeping troops in Afghanistan combat zones.

Dutton said the British contribution is "significant," as well as that of Canada, which he noted has lost more troops per capita in Afghanistan than any other nation.

Nicholson, the U.S. general, said the Canadians have fought "heroically" but simply don't have enough forces to secure all of Kandahar. The Canadian Embassy declined to comment.

Fighting should eventually clear the way for security and governance to take hold.

More U.S. troops—151—died in Afghanistan in 2008 than any of the seven years since the invasion to oust the Taliban, and U.S. officials warn violence will probably intensify next year.

"If we get the troops, they're going to move into areas that haven't been secured, and when we do that, the enemy is there, and we're going to fight," said Nicholson, who spent 16 months commanding a brigade of 10th Mountain Division troops in eastern Afghanistan in 2006 and 2007.

That fighting should eventually clear the way for security and governance to take hold, he said.

"If you want to summarize that as it's going to get worse before it gets better, that's exactly what we're talking about," he said.

An Expanded U.S. Military Effort in Afghanistan May Be Exactly What al-Qaeda Wants

Paul Rogers

Paul Rogers is professor of peace studies at Bradford University in northern England. He is openDemocracy's international-security editor; his weekly column for the site has been published since September 2001. He is a consultant to the Oxford Research Group, for which he produces a monthly security briefing. Among his books are Losing Control *(Pluto Press, 3rd ed. [forthcoming], 2009);* A War Too Far: Iraq, Iran and the New American Century *(Pluto Press, 2006);* Global Security and the War on Terror: Elite Power and the Illusion of Control *(Routledge, 2007); and* Why We're Losing the War on Terror *(Polity, 2008).*

The Taliban's [a fundamentalist Islamic militia] sophisticated, deadly new tactics are bringing the group closer to Kabul [Afghanistan's capital]. The United States' response is to redouble the failed tactics that helped achieve this outcome.

Many sober analysts of the war in Afghanistan expected a military offensive by the Taliban in the early months of 2008. They also suspected that Taliban paramilitaries would avoid major confrontations with foreign forces, out of awareness of the overwhelming firepower that these could launch even on quite small groups. They expected instead an extension of the use of small raids, improvised roadside-bombs and suicide-attacks.

In the event these tactics have indeed been widely used. But the increased level of Taliban activity has been expressed in many other ways as well. They have included a closely co-ordinated assault on a prison in Kandahar that released hun-

Paul Rogers, "Afghanistan: On the Cliff-Edge," *openDemocracy*, August 31, 2008. Reproduced by permission.

dreds of Taliban detainees; an attack on the Serena international hotel in the heart of Kabul on 14 January [2008]; the bombing of the Indian embassy there on 7 July [2008]; and a major increase in attacks on transport links [on] 14 August 2008.

This widening of targets is serious enough for American, British and other military commanders. What has really surprised them, however, has been the ability of Taliban and other militias to engage in significant conventional military attacks. One of these, on 13 July [2008], killed nine United States troops in a newly established but isolated base in Kunar province; another, on 19 August [2008], killed ten French soldiers in Sarbi district, only fifty kilometres east of Kabul. The deteriorating situation in Afghanistan had even before these assaults been reflected in the redeployment of a full aircraft-carrier battle-group led by the *USS Abraham Lincoln* to the Indian Ocean to bring its planes within range of southern Afghanistan.

The result is to provide the US with far more airpower. In addition, the group's flagship has offered itself as a venue for high-level diplomacy: top US and Pakistani military commanders (including Admiral Mike Mullen, chairman of the US joint chiefs-of-staff, and General Ashfaq Kayani, the Pakistan army's chief-of-staff) met on the *USS Abraham Lincoln* on 26 August [2008] to analyse the security crisis in Afghanistan and Pakistan itself—without, it seems, a positive result.

Taliban militias, along with warlord groups and al-Qaida paramilitaries, have considerably expanded their influence across much of . . . Afghanistan.

By the last week of August 2008, the total US military death-toll in Afghanistan has reached 580; as many as 105 have been killed in 2008 alone, including sixty-five in May-July, the worst period since the war started in October 2001.

Across the border in Pakistan, there were credible reports of an expanding Taliban/al-Qaida training system, with new camps established in the border districts. Some limited Pakistani army actions had very little effect, while sixty-four people were killed in a double bombing of one of Pakistan's largest munitions factories.

An Argument of Force

There is now a developing consensus that Taliban militias, along with warlord groups and al-Qaida [an international terrorist network led by Osama bin Laden] paramilitaries, have considerably expanded their influence across much of southern and southeastern Afghanistan, with Taliban/al-Qaida elements also gaining control of large areas of western Pakistan close to the Afghan border. A deep concern over the vulnerability of the major military supply-routes from the Pakistani port of Karachi through to Kabul has been compounded by a Russian threat to suspend its agreement with NATO [North Atlantic Treaty Organization, an alliance of European and North American countries] for transit of military materials through its own territory.

The coalition's reliance on air-power has resulted in further civilian casualties. Around 700 Afghan civilians have been killed in January-August 2008; the worst such incident being on 21 August when, according to United Nations sources, at least sixty children and thirty adults were killed in a US air-raid. Meanwhile, Taliban units are now operating close to Kabul, and have advanced to secure control of parts of Kandahar.

From the Pentagon's perspective, what is to be done? Most of the foreign forces in Afghanistan are under NATO control in the International Security Assistance Force (ISAF); but this is largely under the leadership of the United States, and the overall war in Afghanistan is dominated by US planning and support. Britain, together with Canada and the Netherlands, may be heavily involved in counter-insurgency operations, but they are relatively small actors in a scene where the Pentagon is the driving-force.

There is only one answer to the Taliban revival, the revitalisation of al-Qaida, and even the jihadist *presence in western Pakistan: the application of intense military force.*

Thus, the views of Washington are decisive: and the overwhelming judgment there—across the political spectrum—is that Afghanistan is now the central focus of the "war on terror". The John McCain and Barack Obama camps [during the 2008 presidential election] each [took] . . . the view that there must be a substantial increase in the use of military force in Afghanistan, especially if some limited withdrawals from Iraq become possible.

A Game of Consequence

Thus, the bottom-line is that there is only one answer to the Taliban revival, the revitalisation of al-Qaida, and even the *jihadist* [those espousing "holy war"] presence in western Pakistan: the application of intense military force. There is simply no other way.

This has three key consequences. The first is that the more force that is applied in Afghanistan the greater the risk not just of civilian casualties but of creating an environment in which the foreign military presence is seen more and more as an occupation. There are already well over 60,000 foreign troops in the country, with the majority engaged in combat. Moreover, civilian deaths are causing such controversy that Kabul's political class is trying to distance itself from the United States. As a military build-up intensifies in late 2008, there is a strong risk that the perception of occupation will extend well beyond the Taliban and other militias together with their immediate supporters.

The second consequence is that the more a perception of western occupation grows, the more likely it is that the opposing forces take on a perspective of global *jihad*. Most previous resistance to foreign forces, as against the Soviets in the 1980s, was grounded in nationalist or ethnic sentiment rather than being part of a global movement. Over the past year there have been clear signs that Taliban militias in conjunction with the al-Qaida movement and paramilitaries that have travelled from north Africa, the middle east and central Asia have increasingly seen their insurgency as elements in just such a movement.

The more force that is applied in Afghanistan the greater the risk not just of civilian casualties but of creating an environment in which the foreign military presence is seen . . . as an occupation.

Moreover, the impulses of sympathy with these radical forces are fuelled by the detailed reporting by *al-Jazeera* [an Arabic news network] and other media outlets of the many civilian victims of western air-strikes and other calamities in Afghanistan. This ensures that Muslims across the rest of the world are becoming as aware of what is happening in Afghanistan as they have been regarding Iraq since 2003.

The third consequence is the state of Pakistan, where political instability and the resignation of [president] Pervez Musharraf entails a decrease in United States influence over actions in the border districts. Many of these districts are independent of Islamabad's [Pakistan's capital] control, paramilitary training-camps are operating, supplies readily pass through to Afghanistan, and supportive populations provide a stream of recruits to the cause across the border. Almost all military analysts agree that the subjugation of the Taliban and associated warlords in Afghanistan is impossible as long as this situation continues. The al-Qaida leadership has also sufficiently reconstituted itself in western Pakistan to be able once more to exert influence even beyond the middle east and southwest Asia.

A Bitter Harvest

The impact of these developments on the United States is to increase the conviction that to win the war in Afghanistan requires the application of greater force there and an acceptance that at some stage the US will have to intervene forcefully in western Pakistan. There are alternatives, including an acceptance of the need to engage systematically with some of the less radical militia elements, but these are simply not on Washington's agenda. Thus a more intense and more extensive war seems likely between now and early 2010, with the likelihood that this is just what the al-Qaida movement wants.

In 2003, a few analysts warned that occupying Iraq would lead to an intense and dangerous conflict that would serve as a *jihadist* combat training-zone of great value to the al-Qaida movement. That was indeed the outcome; and an American insistence on remaining in Iraq—whatever the Nouri al-Maliki [Iraq's Prime Minister] government may want—means that Iraq may yet come to the fore in this role again. For now, though, the focus moves on—or more correctly, back—to Afghanistan.

Osama bin Laden and the other elements of the al-Qaida leadership may well be looking forward to a new era in their conflict with their "far enemy."

When the nineteen hijackers perpetrated the 9/11 atrocities [in 2001], the al-Qaida movement no doubt expected that the United States would occupy Afghanistan and could be vanquished there in a war of grinding attrition, just as the Soviets had been. In the event, to terminate the Taliban regime the Pentagon cleverly used air-power, special forces and a re-arming of the Northern Alliance rather than a direct occupation.

Even then, this seemed to be too easy. One of the earliest columns in this series suggested that: ". . . an apparent US victory achieved before the end of the year may, in reality, be just a further stage in a longer-term civil war in Afghanistan. This is supported by the likelihood that many Taliban and al-Qaida units have already crossed the border into north-west Pakistan, where there is substantial local support for their position . . ."

Now that a direct occupation of Afghanistan has evolved and is set to expand, there is the added complication of deep insecurity across the border in Pakistan. Only two months away from the eighth year of the start of the Afghan war—and following their recent setbacks in Iraq—Osama bin Laden and the other elements of the al-Qaida leadership may well be looking forward to a new era in their conflict with their "far enemy". Iraq has to an extent served its purpose, but Afghanistan may now come to overshadow even that bitter and costly conflict.

Sending More U.S. Troops to Afghanistan Will Likely Create Another Iraq War

Mark Vorpahl

Mark Vorpahl is an anti-war activist and writer for Workers Action, a socialist organization.

While the anti-war movement has primarily targeted the Iraq occupation in its protests and events, opposition to the Afghanistan occupation has always been understood as a shared point of agreement among the vast majority of participants. The Afghanistan occupation has been not as prominent in the minds of protesters because of fewer lives lost and less money wasted than in Iraq. Recent developments, however, indicate that this could be changing.

A U.S. Troop Surge

On December 20 [2008], U.S. Joint Chief of Staff Admiral Mike Mullen announced the intention of sending 30,000 more U.S. troops to Afghanistan by next summer. This would be in addition to the 31,000 U.S. troops already in Afghanistan as well as 35,000 other Allied troops under NATO [North Atlantic Treaty Organization, an alliance of European and North American countries] command. This represents a dramatic escalation of U.S. involvement in Afghanistan not only in terms of numbers, but also in the speed-up of the timeline for sending in more troops. Previously, Pentagon spokesmen had said it would be 18 months before any new military personnel were sent over in full force. Now Admiral Mullen has stated there will be a far greater number of soldiers sent to Afghanistan than mentioned before, and in as little as six months.

The reason for this escalation is because the occupation has been failing when confronted by a growing opposition that is becoming more sophisticated in combating the foreign occupying troops. 2008 has been the most violent year since the Taliban [a fundamentalist Islamic militia] government was toppled in 2001, with a 25 percent increase in soldiers' deaths who were under NATO or the U.S. command. Recently, Taliban attacks have succeeded in disrupting the route that carries up to 75 percent of supplies to the foreign forces. For all their greater military technology, the U.S. is proving to be outmatched by a homegrown insurgency that is determined to kick the occupiers out.

Consequently, the power brokers in Washington have decided to dedicate more resources to defeat them—but at what cost to U.S. citizens? Currently, the Afghanistan occupation is costing U.S. tax payers $2 billion a month. The increase advocated by Admiral Mullen is expected, by some, to nearly double this amount, totaling $3.5 billion per month.

There can be little doubt that President [Barack] Obama was consulted about this escalation as he prepare[d] to take over the Executive Office. Admiral Mullen has stated that the increase of soldiers in Afghanistan would be tied to a withdrawal of troops from Iraq. In what way it is tied remains unclear since the newest military plan envisions a withdrawal of no more than 8,000 troops from Iraq within the first six months of 2009. However, even if many more troops are withdrawn from Iraq, millions of U.S. citizens did not vote for Obama to jump from one quagmire to another. They wanted to see an end to U.S. involvement in all unjust, unwinnable, and colossally wasteful wars. Though Obama never made it a secret that he favored greater involvement in Afghanistan and even stated that he would be willing to authorize military strikes in Pakistan in pursuit of Afghan rebels, he was voted in as a "peace candidate" because many wishfully believed he would reverse the war policies of Bush. The surge of troops in Afghanistan that Obama will preside over, will be the first significant challenge to this popular perception.

Currently, the Afghanistan occupation is costing U.S. tax payers $2 billion a month. The increase [in troops] . . . is expected, by some, to nearly double this amount.

[Former President George W.] Bush, [2008 presidential candidate Senator John] McCain, and Obama have all stated that the reason for the U.S. war and occupation of Afghanistan is to fight terrorism. Yet the effect of both the Iraq and Afghanistan occupations has been to embolden and strengthen the forces the U.S. has labeled as terrorists—that is, anyone who would use military means to fight for their national sovereignty. The escalation of U.S. troops in Afghanistan will likely see a corresponding strengthening of the Taliban and other militias as more Afghan civilians suffer under the occupation and are willing to support anyone that can fight against it. This will have destabilizing effects throughout the entire region.

The Real Reason the United States Is in Afghanistan

In reality, the aim of "fighting terrorism" is only for public relations consumption. There are stronger economic and geopolitical motivations at work behind the Afghanistan occupation that bear no relation to the sound bites fed to the American people. These motivations revolve around the need of U.S. big business to assert its economic and political control over Central Asia's energy resources against all potential competitors. The number of lives lost and the devastating horrors spread as a result of the war are an unpleasant but tolerable consequence to the players of this deadly chess game who are focused on the pursuit of their own narrow self interests, namely profits.

The central reason behind the Afghanistan war and occupation is to gain control over an oil and natural gas transit route that can provide Europe with much of its energy, and to contain the influence of Russia, China, and Iran in the region. While all these powers are attempting to take advantage of the occupation by appearing to co-operate with the US, there is no more honor behind this cooperation than there is in a den of thieves planning a heist while each, behind the backs of their cohorts, tries to figure out how to snatch the lion's share of stolen goods.

This becomes obvious when examining the economically based politics behind the proposed U.S. supply routes to Afghanistan, as is discussed in the article "All Roads Lead Out of Afghanistan" by former India ambassador MK Bhadrakumer. Aside from the current Karachi routes that the Taliban and others have been attacking with growing success, there are three other possibilities. One starts at the port of Shanghai, and goes across China, through Tajikistan, to reach Afghanistan. Another takes a land route through Russia, Kazakhstan, Uzbekistan/Turkmenistan to reach the Afghan border. The third and shortest goes straight through Iran.

Instead of using these routes, which would strengthen the political hand of the nations they pass through, the U.S. is planning to build another from scratch. The plan is to use the Black Sea port of Poti in Georgia, and then take the cargo through Georgia, Azerbaijan, Kazakhstan, and Uzbekistan to the Afghan border. According to MK Bhadrakumer:

> The project, if it materializes, will be a geopolitical coup—
> the biggest ever that Washington would have swung in post-
> Soviet Central Asia and the Caucasus. At one stroke, the
> U.S. will be tying up military cooperation at the bilateral
> level with Azerbaijan, Kazakhstan, Uzbekistan and Turk-

menistan. Furthermore, the U.S. will be effectively drawing these countries closer into NATO's partnership programs. Georgia, in particular, gets a privileged status as the key transit country, which will offset the current European opposition to its induction as a NATO member country. Besides, the U.S. will have virtually dealt a blow to the Russia-led Collective Security Treaty Organization (CSTO) and the Shanghai Cooperation Organization (SCO). Not only will the U.S. have succeeded in keeping the CSTO and the SCO from poking their noses into the Afghan cauldron, it will also have made these organizations largely irrelevant to regional security when Kazakhstan and Uzbekistan, the two key players in Central Asia, simply step out of the ambit of these organizations and directly deal with the U.S. and NATO.

The central reason behind the Afghanistan war and occupation is to gain control over an oil and natural gas transit route that can provide Europe with much of its energy.

The creation of this route would also establish the U.S. as a long term military presence in the South Caucasus. This will be much to the distress of Russia which would correctly view this as a threat to their own interests and, potentially, their national security. This route is the prize because it could also be easily converted into an energy corridor, as was mentioned, for supplying the European market. This would greatly harm Russia's and Iran's business dealings with Europe, as well as make European policy more dependent on U.S. interests.

This policy, with its lucrative prospects, is in large part behind the escalation of U.S. troops in Afghanistan. Those business-directed government officials that are pursuing this policy are so far removed from the lives that will be destroyed by the lust for profits and so consumed with defending the interests of a tiny minority of big business owners that they are blind to the larger international social impact of their strategies and the consequences this impact unleashes.

A Likelihood of Failure

A military victory in Afghanistan is even more unlikely than it is in Iraq—which is not going so well and many believe is failing. This is partly because the Afghan population is not centered in large cities, but scattered across a mountainous landscape, ideal for guerrilla warfare. The British and the Russians learned this the hard way in their attempts to occupy this nation. The Taliban have been fighting in this terrain for decades and know it well. They also are emboldened by knowing that whenever a foreign power has tried to hold Afghanistan by force, they have always left in defeat.

The U.S. is attempting to bribe the warlords of local militias in order to win them over to fighting on the occupier's side. While this may have some initial success, it will blow up in the U.S. government's face. Each of these warlords are guided by their own interests, quite distinct and often opposed to each other's, not to mention U.S. long term goals. The only way that the U.S. can succeed in Afghanistan is to set up a state that will defend U.S. interests. But this will prove to be an impossible task since any state, by definition, requires a consolidated force of armed bodies. However, combining these scattered and feuding militias into a centralized, cohesive force on the basis of defending U.S. interests is simply not feasible. More likely, the building up of these militias will create a monster like Frankenstein's just as the U.S. training and funding of the Mujahadeen during the Russian occupation in Afghanistan helped to create [Osama] Bin Laden [leader of al Qaeda, an international terrorist network].

The escalation of U.S. troops in Afghanistan will produce a destructive fallout across the whole Central Asian region. The occupation has already greatly contributed to destabilizing the political situation in Pakistan. Though not directly related, the recent attacks in Mumbai, India can only be understood in the context of the militancy radiating from the Afghan war. Considering the explosive situation in the region, sending more troops into Afghanistan could have the effect of pouring gasoline on a fire.

A military victory in Afghanistan is even more unlikely than it is in Iraq.

On an even more menacing scale, the growing military presence could draw the U.S. into a war with more formidable powers such as Russia, China, or Iran. This is especially the case during a period of international economic crisis. Profits are shrinking for each nation's corporations and banks. Even with shrinking profits, each nation's government is nevertheless duty bound to make sure their ruling class' enterprises remain viable and positioned to get ahead of their competitors. They cannot do this by encouraging more production and flooding the international market with an excessive amount of goods. There are too few consumers who can afford to buy these commodities at a price that would leave the capitalists with a profit. Therefore, each government is compelled to employ policies that hurt the profit and productive capacity of their competitors in order to be on top of a declining ability to raise their domestic profits.

This is indicated by the U.S. government's attempts to circumvent the established supply routes running through Russia, China, or Iran. While using one of these established routes would be more efficient, the U.S. is more concerned with not allowing its international competitors to take advantage of the construction that has already been done since this would give them an edge against the U.S. in the region. Such a state of affairs tends to take on a gathering momentum with unforeseen consequences for the policy makers. While no U.S. official would now be in favor of a war with Russia or China, and few would support one with Iran, the logic of the Afghanistan occupation combined with the international economic crisis could propel things in this direction.

The escalation of U.S. troops in Afghanistan, the continuing war in Iraq, and all the potential effects of spreading instability and more war is beginning to hit the American public hard. They voted for Obama in hopes for a change. However, as a capitalist Democratic Party politician, he has no more ability to fundamentally reverse course than a pig has the ability to fly. As unemployment soars, pensions collapse, health care rots, and the social safety net gets hacked away, the astronomical cost of the U.S. wars and occupations will leave more people questioning the viability of the system we live under. People will begin to pointedly ask, "Why do the politicians spend so much on destruction rather than production? Why are the rich bailed out, but not the workers?" And these thoughts will be expressed by many more people. When a system can no longer provide for its people, while vast amounts of resources are spent on wasteful destructive adventures, then that system is in all likelihood doomed.

It will take a mass, working class-led movement to make any real change. . . . Especially in light of the escalation in Afghanistan, too much is at stake to passively wish Obama will change things. We must mobilize to shout in as large a collective voice as possible, "End the War and Occupation in Iraq & Afghanistan Now!"

The Afghanistan War Looms as a Potential Quagmire

Michael Crowley

Michael Crowley is an American journalist and a senior editor for The New Republic, *a progressive magazine.*

Around the time of the November election, John Nagl, a retired [U.S.] Army Colonel, took a helicopter ride across Afghanistan. What he saw below worried him. Nagl, who is 42 with trim brown hair and academic eyeglasses, spent three years in Iraq, including as part of a tank battalion in the Sunni Triangle, where he witnessed brutal combat in the war's worst years. A West Point graduate and Rhodes Scholar, Nagl applied the lessons of his Iraq experience to the *Army-Marine Counterinsurgency Field Manual*, which he helped write and which was published last year. He currently specializes in the study of war and counterinsurgency at the Center for a New American Security, a center-left Washington think tank, and it is in this capacity that he recently traveled to the Afghan war zone. As his military chopper swooped over high mountain ridges and plunging valleys, he grimly surveyed the size and the inhospitality of the Afghan terrain. Winning in Afghanistan, he realized, would take more than "a little tweak," as he put it to me from back in Washington a few weeks later, when he was still shaking off the gritty "Kabul crud" that afflicts traveler's lungs. It would take time, money, and blood. "It's a doubling of the U.S. commitment," Nagl said. "It's a doubling of the Afghan army, maybe a tripling. It's going to require a tax increase and a bigger army."

The Challenge of Winning the War in Afghanistan

For the left in the [former President George W.] Bush era, America's two wars have long been divided into the good and the bad. Iraq was the moral and strategic catastrophe, while Afghanistan—home base for the September 11 [2001] attacks—was a righteous fight. This dichotomy was especially appealing to liberals because it allowed them to pair their call for withdrawal from Iraq with a call for escalation in Afghanistan. Leaving Iraq wasn't about retreating; it was about bolstering another front, one where our true strategic interests lie. The left could meet conservative charges of defeatism with the rhetoric of victory. [U.S. President] Barack Obama is now getting ready to turn this idea into policy. He has already called for sending an additional two U.S. brigades, or roughly 10,000 troops, to the country and may wind up proposing a much larger escalation in what candidate Obama has called "the war we need to win."

But, as Nagl understands at the ground level, winning in Afghanistan will take more than just shifting a couple of brigades from the bad war to the good one. Securing Afghanistan—and preserving a government and society we can be proud of—is vastly more challenging than the rhetoric of the campaign has suggested. Taliban [a fundamentalist Islamic militia] fighters are bolder and crueler than ever—beheading dozens of men at a time, blasting the capital with car bombs, killing NATO [North Atlantic Treaty Organization, an alliance of European and North American countries] troops with sniper fire and roadside explosives. Meanwhile, the recent savagery in Mumbai has India and Pakistan at each other's throats again, a development that indirectly benefits Afghan insurgents.

The challenge of exiting Iraq was supposed to be the first great foreign policy test of Obama's presidency. But it is Afghanistan that now looms as the potential quagmire. Winning the good war will, at a minimum, require the most sophisticated counterinsurgency techniques developed by Nagl and his colleagues, which take enormous resources. But, even then, it's not at all clear what victory looks like, or whether it's even possible in a country known as the graveyard of empires. All of which raises the question of how much longer Afghanistan really can be considered the good war. . . .

Difficult Questions

On May 23, 2005 George W. Bush welcomed Afghanistan's president, Hamid Karzai to Washington. As the two leaders met the press in the White House's East Room, Bush praised his counterpart as a beacon of freedom and democracy. "I am honored to stand by the first democratically elected leader in the five-thousand-year history of Afghanistan. Congratulations," Bush rhapsodized.

Afghanistan earned its status as the "good war" not just because it was a direct response to the September 11 attacks, but because—unlike in Iraq—it quickly produced an affable, Westernized leader who was the product of a democratic process. But times have changed. Public disapproval among Afghans of Karzai's weak and corruption-rife government has doubled in the past year, according to a summer [2008] poll by the Asia Foundation. Karzai himself is now viewed as ineffectual, corrupt, or both. His brother has been implicated in heroin trafficking on a massive scale. And, now, the West is considering its alternatives. According to a leaked diplomatic cable recently published by a French newspaper, the British ambassador to Afghanistan has declared the country in "crisis," and thinks the "realistic" solution is the installation of "an acceptable dictator." For many Afghanistan-watchers, such an outcome would be no surprise. "I can only laugh" at Bush's dreams of democracy, says Les Gelb of the Council on Foreign Relations. "It's in our bones as Americans to think that we can democratize those societies. It's a vast cultural ignorance."

Barack Obama may well agree. When talking about the importance of Afghanistan, he does so in strategic, not moral, terms. Gone is Bush's swooning rhetoric of democracy and human rights. To hear Obama tell it, Afghanistan is the "central front" against terrorists, and possibly the place where Osama bin Laden [leader of al Qaeda, an international terrorist network] can be found. In July [2008], Obama told a McClatchy reporter that America's goals in the country should be "relatively modest," adding that "[o]ur critical goal should be to make sure that the Taliban and Al Qaeda are routed and that they cannot project threats against us from that region."

But even this "relatively modest" goal necessitates that Obama weigh in on some morally complex—and interrelated—questions. One is whether a weakened Karzai is more of a hindrance to the goal of stamping out insurgents than an asset. With Afghanistan due to hold a national election in late 2009, some regional experts believe that Obama should pull the plug on the increasingly unpopular and ineffective leader. "I think Karzai should get the boot," says Marvin Weinbaum, a regional expert and former [Bill] Clinton and Bush State Department official now with the Middle East Institute. "As long as he's around, there can't be anything in the way of a fresh start." Even if Obama agrees with this assessment—and judging from the fact that he waited nearly three weeks after the election to speak to Karzai, he may well—he faces the problem of finding a credible alternative.

The challenge of exiting Iraq was supposed to be the first great foreign policy test of Obama's presidency. But it is Afghanistan that now looms as the potential quagmire.

Another question is whether to strike a deal with the Taliban. Almost everyone who looks hard at Afghanistan concludes that some kind of political settlement will be required to end the stubborn insurgency. General David Petraeus, fresh from his apparent success in Iraq and now commander of Central Command, is shifting his focus to Afghanistan and the question of whether it's possible to negotiate with moderate elements of the Taliban in hopes of replicating something like Iraq's Sunni Awakening, which co-opted Sunni tribes in Anbar province and turned them against Al Qaeda.

Easier said than done. The Sunnis turned against Al Qaeda because they were foreign interlopers—whereas the Taliban are largely drawn from Afghanistan's native Pashtun population. Indeed, when Karzai recently offered safe passage to negotiations for the one-eyed Taliban leader Mullah Omar, he was rewarded with mockery by a Taliban spokesman who said the mullah was plenty safe already and moreover quite pleased with the current state of affairs.

Almost everyone who looks hard at Afghanistan concludes that some kind of political settlement [with the Taliban] will be required to end the stubborn insurgency.

It's also not clear who the United States should be talking *to*. A recent report by the [think tank] Center for American Progress names six major Islamic insurgent groups fighting in Afghanistan—including not just the Taliban and Al Qaeda but a colorful cast of characters, such as the Islamic movement of Uzbekistan; the so-called "Haqqani Network," which recently tried to kill Karzai; and Hezb-i-Islami Gulbuddin, followers of the rapacious Afghan warlord and former bin Laden ally Gulbuddin Hekmatyar, who once declared that, because a million Afghans had already died in civil wars there, he saw no great problem with another million perishing. The Taliban itself consists of numerous tribally oriented splinter groups with various leaders and motivations—some little more than criminal gangs who may be willing to cooperate with the United States for the right price. But the group's core leadership is not the deal-making kind. "When I was at the State Department, we had some dealings with [the Omar-led Taliban], and it always came down to 'We've got time and Allah on our side,'" says Weinbaum.

If Taliban leaders were to accept a deal, it would probably involve granting them real power. "We have to begin to think about the possibility of the Taliban in some fashion coming back to power," says Gelb. Deterrence—the threat of a massive post-September-11-like retaliation for any terror attack originating from the country—could prevent Al Qaeda from setting up shop again, Gelb argues.

But could Obama—could the United States—stomach what would be essentially reinstalling the Taliban to power? A central moral element of the "good war" was the liberation of millions of Afghan women subject to the Taliban's harsh *sharia* law, which prevented girls from being educated, chopped off fingers with painted nails, and stoned women for adultery and executed others at midfield of a newly-constructed soccer stadium in front of thousands. Shortly after the fall of the Taliban, in November 2001, Hillary Clinton, soon to be Obama's woman at Foggy Bottom [the U.S. Department of State] and a key voice in the Afghanistan debate, penned a *Time* essay arguing against the notion that imposing Western values there amounted to "cultural imperialism." "Women's rights are human rights," Clinton wrote. "They are not simply American, or western customs."

Stirring words, to be sure. But the day may come when cutting deals in Afghanistan means consigning some women, if not to the brutal life of the high Taliban era, to strict Islamic rules sure to offend the likes of Hillary Clinton. It may well be, in other words, that America's moral and strategic interests are beginning to diverge in Afghanistan in a way that supporters of the "good war" may not yet appreciate.

Fighting Terrorism

Sometime after midnight on Saturday, November 22 [2008], an unmanned U.S. Predator drone slipped through the skies of Pakistan's North Waziristan province and hovered above the small town of Ali Khel. In an instant, three Hellfire missiles launched from the drone and rocketed at 950 miles per hour into a mud hut below. The explosions that lit up the night sky abruptly ended the life of Rashid Rauf, a British Islamic militant believed to have masterminded the 2006 Al Qaeda plot to blow up several transatlantic airliners. Two other senior Al Qaeda operatives were eliminated along with Rauf.

This was just one of the most successful in a recent series of Predator strikes at Taliban and Al Qaeda leaders in the remote tribal areas along Pakistan's border with Afghanistan. Although the Pakistani government privately winks at (but publicly denounces) the Predator strikes, it keeps these areas off-limits to NATO ground troops. And Pakistani forces have made largely halfhearted and ineffectual efforts to root out the Taliban and Al Qaeda leaders—perhaps including bin Laden himself—who hide in the region's mud houses and mountain caves.

The linchpin of Obama's case for escalating the war in Afghanistan is that, unlike Iraq, it's in our strategic interest. But, the closer you look at that premise, the blurrier it can get. The tale of Rauf's demise illustrates that our strategic interest may best be served by focusing on Pakistan. The inconvenient fact is that, since September 11, Pakistan, and not Afghanistan, has emerged as Al Qaeda's true home. "Al Qaeda isn't in Afghanistan, they're in *Pakistan*," says Kenneth Pollack [of the Brookings Institution]. Pakistan offers the Taliban sanctuary, which in turn allows Taliban fighters to escape annihilation by NATO forces who can't chase them across the border. Adds Pollack: "It's clear that you cannot solve the problems of Afghanistan without solving Pakistan."

But "solving" Pakistan is an entirely different project than winning in Afghanistan. It is a matter of diplomacy and foreign aid, not large contingents of ground troops. It requires boosting the economy of a country now teetering near bankruptcy. And it entails, as Obama's team has acknowledged, a new push to soothe the extreme tensions between Islamic Pakistan and its Hindu rival, India. Hatred for India foments radicalism on the margins of Pakistani society. And it leads Pakistan's notorious intelligence services to provide support for the Taliban, which it sees as a buffer against creeping Indian influence within Afghanistan. . . .

The inconvenient fact is that, since September 11, Pakistan, and not Afghanistan, has emerged as Al Qaeda's true home.

Meanwhile, it's quite possible that a major U.S. troop buildup in another Muslim nation is just what Al Qaeda wants. In mid-November [2008], the senior Al Qaeda commander Ayman Al Zawahiri released a message for Barack Obama. In addition to slurring Obama as a "house negro" and gloating over the coming U.S. exit from Iraq, he said that Obama's plan to "pull your troops out of Iraq to send them to Afghanistan is a policy which was destined for failure before it was born." "[R]emember the fate of Bush and [former Pakistani President] Pervez Musharraf, and the fate of the Soviets and British before them. And be aware that the dogs of Afghanistan have found the flesh of your soldiers to be delicious, so send thousands after thousands to them."

Yes, this was the ranting of a deranged terrorist. But, if the United States really does leave Iraq, Al Qaeda will turn Afghanistan into its next recruiting tool. Even among the Afghan people, sending foreign forces might simply have a backlash effect. "We run the risk that our military presence . . . will gradually turn the Afghan population entirely against us," former national security adviser—and sometime Obama adviser—Zbigniew Brzezinski told the *Financial Times* this summer [2008].

All of this raises the question of whether a major troop escalation is truly worth the costs. According to a recent *Washington Post* report, military planners are debating whether a smaller U.S. contingent, based around Special Forces and military trainers for Afghan security forces, and complemented by Predator drones, can achieve a reduced set of U.S. goals—namely, preventing Al Qaeda from reconstituting.

When I asked John Nagl about such a scenario, he bristled at the thought. Nagl still believes that Afghanistan is a good war for both moral and strategic reasons. "I think that, without a very substantial commitment to the government of Afghanistan, there's a very real chance that the Taliban returns to power there," he says. "I think that would not be good for the stability of the government of Pakistan. And I am personally unwilling to let a regime that throws acid in the faces of little girls who go to school take power."

It's quite possible that a major U.S. troop buildup in another Muslim nation is just what Al Qaeda wants.

Hard Choices

But just because Afghanistan may be a good war doesn't mean it will be an easy one. Nagl warns that, in order to win, we need to approach the situation there with our eyes wide open. Obama will need to move beyond the rhetoric of the good war to convey to the American public the sacrifice and hard choices of war itself. "If resources are limited," Nagl says, then Obama should "mobilize the country"—increase the size of the military and even ask Americans to pay more through taxes. "How badly do we want to win this war to ensure that nobody can use this territory to kill three thousand Americans again?" he asks. "I'm willing to pay an extra dollar a gallon of gas for that to happen—who's with me?"

We'll soon find out. Nagl's instincts may be right. The case for rescuing Afghanistan with great military force and at vast expense may carry the day. No one can dispute that the world would be a better place if Afghanistan is peaceful, stable, and at least semi-democratic. But, as one painful war winds down and a deep recession strikes, it's unclear whether Americans are prepared to make the necessary sacrifices. Ultimately Obama, and the United States, may find that the goodness of this war isn't good—or simple—enough.

The War in Afghanistan Will Be Another Vietnam

Alan Caruba

Alan Caruba is a writer for WesternFront America, a Web site dedicated to Americanism, conservatism, free enterprise, life, liberty, and individualism.

The next President of the United States of America must decide whether to withdraw our troops from Afghanistan or expand our involvement there. Having lived through the long years of the war in Vietnam, I can tell you that Afghanistan looks and smells like Vietnam. It is the classic wrong war in the wrong place.

A Primitive Place

In late October [2008], I read a small news item about Parwiz Kambakhsh, 24, an Afghan journalism student who had downloaded and circulated an article about women's rights under Islam. The news was that his sentence of death had been overturned by an appellate court that reduced it to a mere twenty years in prison on the charge of blasphemy. He can still appeal to the Supreme Court of Afghanistan. This is the state of freedom of speech, press, and thought in Afghanistan.

If you want to know what life was like in the seventh century, Afghanistan is the place to go. It is largely devoid of anything passing for modernity, by which we mean medical facilities, schools, roads, and such. Never mind the telephones and other detritus of modern life, the conversations have not changed in centuries.

Afghanistan shares a long border with Pakistan and Iran. Also bordering it is Turkmenistan, Uzbekistan, Turkistan, and Tajikistan. None of these places is a tourist destination. All are Islamic.

Alan Caruba, "Afghanistan Will Be Another Vietnam," AnxietyCenter.com, November 2, 2008. Reproduced by permission.

The only reliable element of Afghanistan's economy is poppy cultivation for the opium trade which the CIA [the U.S. Central Intelligence Agency] estimates generates "roughly $4 billion in illicit economic activity." This is another way of saying that none of this money reaches what passes for a central government except in the form of bribes. It is a major source of funding for the Taliban [a fundamentalist Islamic militia].

Much like the "military advisors" that initiated our involvement in Vietnam, today's generals are calling for more troops [in Afghanistan].

The Folly of Sending More Troops

Few Americans were interested in Afghanistan until [the terrorist attacks on the United States on] September 11, 2001. We have had military presence there for seven years, along with NATO [North Atlantic Treaty Organization, an alliance of European and North American countries] nation components. Much like the "military advisors" that initiated our involvement in Vietnam, today's generals are calling for more troops.

Afghanistan has been conquered and occupied since the days of Alexander the Great. Nothing much comes of it. It remains a mystery why they bothered. Putting too few or too many troops into Afghanistan does little except to demonstrate the futility of trying to impose one's will on people who have resisted every such effort for centuries.

Founded as a nation in 1747 when Ahmad Shah Durrani unified the Pashtun tribes, Afghanistan was primarily seen as a buffer between the British and Russian empires. Democracy, as in most Middle Eastern nations, has never taken root there.

It became the graveyard of the Soviet empire after they intervened militarily in 1979 to support a tottering Afghan Communist regime. After they withdrew in 1989, the Soviet Union collapsed in 1991. It is now known as the Russian Federation. It is still run by the former KGB [the intelligence agency of the former Soviet Union]. And one wonders why anyone in the U.S. government thinks any good can come of being there?

The Taliban took control after the Russians left and Osama bin Laden [leader of al-Qaeda, an international terrorist network] found a congenial place in which to plan 9/11. That's why the first U.S. response to the attack occurred in Afghanistan as U.S., allied, and an anti-Taliban Northern Alliance of tribes were able to drive the Taliban across the border into the frontier provinces of Pakistan and elsewhere.

[U.S. President] Barack Obama says that Afghanistan is the "central front" against al Qaeda . . . [but] it has no bases there.

A Lost Cause

The U.S. effort to create a democratic government there began with a new constitution and, in December 2004, the election of Hamid Karzai as president. He barely controls Kabul, the capital. The southern and eastern regions are still beyond control.

In essence, the rule of law barely exists in Afghanistan, if at all, unless you factor in Sharia law [Islamic religious law] which reflects a seventh century approach to justice. The government and all aspects of official life in Afghanistan are so corrupt that even President Karzai's brother is allegedly on the take.

I am not a military strategist, an expert in foreign affairs, or can lay claim to much more than common sense, so I confess it defies my understanding why the United States and our NATO allies are in Afghanistan. Expecting democracy to succeed in such a primitive and hostile place seems more a justification for military occupation than anything else. The whole place is tribal.

Other than his distaste for our invasion of Iraq and disposal of Saddam Hussein, it is baffling that [U.S. President] Barack Obama says that Afghanistan is the "central front" against al Qaeda. The CIA says it has no bases there. The Taliban—outsiders just like us—have their own agenda as seen in their effort to render the place a complete and total Islamic hellhole.

Little wonder, therefore, that word keeps getting out that both English and French military leaders regard Afghanistan as virtually beyond any hope without putting a far greater number of troops there. Millions are being spent as it is. Between 2002 and 2007, Germany spent $80 million to reform its police corps. The U.S. has budgeted $800 million for 2008 to assist its security forces.

In early October, General Jean-Louis Geogelin, France's military chief, confirmed that British Brigadier Mark Carleton-Smith remarks that "there is no military solution to the Afghan crisis" reflected his own views. The Brigadier recommended that NATO lower its expectations regarding a happy outcome to the conflict. It was, he said, "unrealistic and probably incredible" to think that the multinational forces in Afghanistan could rid the country of armed bands.

There are two occupations available to the Afghans. One can either be a farmer raising poppies or one can join an armed band, be it either the government's, one's tribe, or the Taliban's.

Expending troops and treasure in Afghanistan . . . is an invitation to repeat . . . all the errors of Vietnam.

In an October 1, 2008 *Christian Science Monitor* article, it was reported that "The U.S. military is working to put a new strategy in place for Afghanistan and Pakistan that could allow it to expand airfields, preposition military forces and equipment, and prepare for a more robust effort soon against Islamist extremists in the region." Four more U.S. brigades are poised to be sent to Afghanistan, including one that will deploy in January [2009].

I have my own military strategy. Let's pull our troops out of Afghanistan and, with their permission, let's keep enough troops in Iraq to ensure that its government can maintain its security and as a deterrent for any conflict Iran might initiate in the region.

The United States of America has a full plate of problems right now. Expending troops and treasure in Afghanistan strikes me as a bad investment in a very nasty place. It is an invitation to repeat . . . all the errors of Vietnam.

The War in Afghanistan Cannot Be Won

Conn Hallinan

Conn Hallinan is a columnist for Foreign Policy in Focus, *an online project of the Institute for Policy Studies that provides analysis of U.S. foreign policy and international affairs.*

Every war has a story line. World War I was "the war to end all wars." World War II was "the war to defeat fascism."

Iraq was sold as a war to halt weapons of mass destruction; then to overthrow Saddam Hussein, then to build democracy. In the end it was a fabrication built on a falsehood and anchored in a fraud.

But Afghanistan is the "good war," aimed at "those who attacked us," in the words of columnist Frank Rich. It is "the war of necessity," asserts the *New York Times*, to roll back the "power of Al Qaeda [an international terrorist network led by Osama bin Laden] and the Taliban [a fundamentalist Islamic militia]."

[U.S. President] Barack Obama [made] the distinction between the "bad war" in Iraq and the "good war" in Afghanistan a centerpiece of his run for the presidency. He proposes ending the war in Iraq and redeploying U.S. military forces in order "to finish the job in Afghanistan."

A recent poll of Afghan[s] . . . found that . . . 74% want negotiations and 54% would support a coalition government that included the Taliban.

Virtually no one in the United States or the North Atlantic Treaty Organization (NATO) calls for negotiating with the

Conn Hallinan, "Afghanistan: Not a Good War," *Foreign Policy in Focus*, July 30, 2008.

Taliban. Even the *New York Times* editorializes that those who want to talk "have deluded themselves."

But the Taliban government did not attack the United States [on September 11, 2001]. Our old ally, Osama bin Laden, did. Al-Qaeda and the Taliban are not the same organization, and no one seems to be listening to the Afghans.

We should be.

What Afghans Say

A recent poll of Afghan sentiment found that, while the majority dislikes the Taliban, 74% want negotiations and 54% would support a coalition government that included the Taliban.

This poll reflects a deeply divided country where most people are sitting on the fence and waiting for the final outcome of the war. Forty percent think the current government of Hamid Karzai, allied with the United States and NATO, will prevail, 19% say the Taliban, and 40% say it is "too early to say."

The weight of [foreign] occupation, and the rising number of civilian deaths, is shifting the resistance toward a war of national liberation.

There is also strong ambivalence about the presence of foreign troops. Only 14% want them out now, but 52% want them out within three to five years. In short, the Afghans don't want a war to the finish.

They also have a far more nuanced view of the Taliban and al-Qaeda. While the majority oppose both groups—13% support the Taliban and 19% al-Qaeda—only 29% see the former organization as "a united political force."

But that view doesn't fit the West's story line of the enemy as a tightly disciplined band of fanatics.

Whither the Taliban

In fact, the Taliban appears to be evolving from a creation of the U.S., Saudi Arabian, and Pakistani intelligence agencies during Afghanistan's war with the Soviet Union, to a polyglot collection of dedicated Islamists to nationalists. Taliban leader Mullah Mohammad Omar told the *Agence France Presse* early this year, "We're fighting to free our country. We are not a threat to the world."

Those are words that should give Obama, *The New York Times*, and NATO pause.

The initial invasion in 2001 was easy because the Taliban had alienated itself from the vast majority of Afghans. But the weight of occupation, and the rising number of civilian deaths, is shifting the resistance toward a war of national liberation.

No foreign power has ever won that battle in Afghanistan.

War Gone Bad

There is no mystery as to why things have gone increasingly badly for the United States and its allies.

As the United States steps up its air war, civilian casualties have climbed steadily over the past two years. Nearly 700 were killed in the first three months of 2008, a major increase over [2007]. In a recent incident, 47 members of a wedding party were killed in Helmand Province. In a society where clan, tribe, and blood feuds are a part of daily life, that single act sowed a generation of enmity.

Anatol Lieven, a professor of war at King's College London, says that a major impetus behind the growing resistance is anger over the death of family members and neighbors.

Lieven says it is as if Afghanistan is "becoming a sort of surreal hunting estate, in which the U.S. and NATO breed the very terrorists they then track down."

Once a population turns against an occupation (or just decides to stay neutral), there are few places in the world where an occupier can win. Afghanistan, with its enormous size and daunting geography, is certainly not one of them.

Writing in *Der Spiegel*, Ullrich Fichter says that glancing at a map in the International Security Assistance Force's (ISAF) [the NATO Coalition fighting in Afghanistan] headquarters outside Kandahar could give one the impression that Afghanistan is under control. "Colorful little flags identify the NATO troops presence throughout the country," Germans in the northeast, Americans in the east, Italians in the West, British and Canadians in the south, with flags from Turkey, the Netherlands, Spain, Lithuania, Australia and Sweden scattered between.

"But the flags are an illusion," he says.

The UN [United Nations] considers one third of the country "inaccessible," and almost half, "high risk." The number of roadside bombs has increased fivefold over 2004, and the number of armed attacks has jumped by a factor of 10. In the first three months of 2008, attacks around Kabul have surged by 70%. The current national government has little presence outside its capital. President Karzai is routinely referred to as "the mayor of Kabul."

According to *Der Spiegel*, the Taliban are moving north toward Kunduz, just as they did in 1994 when they broke out of their base in Kandahar and started their drive to take over the country. The *Asia Times* says the insurgents' strategy is to cut NATO's supply lines from Pakistan and establish a "strategic corridor" from the border to Kabul.

Afghanistan would require at least 400,000 troops to even have a chance of "winning" the war.

The United States and NATO currently have about 60,000 troops in Afghanistan. But many NATO troops are primarily concerned with rebuilding and development—the story that was sold to the European public to get them to support the war—and only secondarily with war fighting.

The Afghan army adds about 70,000 to that number, but only two brigades and one headquarters unit are considered capable of operating on their own.

According to U.S. counter insurgency doctrine, however, Afghanistan would require at least 400,000 troops to even have a chance of "winning" the war. Adding another 10,000 U.S. troops will have virtually no effect.

By any measure, a military "victory" in Afghanistan is simply not possible.

Afghanistan and the Elections

As the situation continue[d] to deteriorate [in 2008], some voices, including those of the Karzai government and both U.S. presidential candidates, advocate[d] expanding the war into Pakistan in a repeat of the invasions of Laos and Cambodia, when the Vietnam War began spinning out of control. Both those invasions were not only a disaster for the invaders. They also led directly to the genocide in Cambodia.

By any measure, a military "victory" in Afghanistan is simply not possible. The only viable alternative is to begin direct negotiations with the Taliban, and to draw in regional powers with a stake in the outcome: Iran, Pakistan, Russia, Turkmenistan, Tajikistan, China, and India.

But to do so will require abandoning our "story" about the Afghan conflict as a "good war." In this new millennium, there are no good wars.

CHAPTER 4

How Can Afghanistan Be Stabilized in the Long Term?

Chapter Preface

The stated goal of the U.S.-led NATO (North Atlantic Treaty Organization) operation in Afghanistan is to stabilize and provide security for Afghanistan by reducing or ending the insurgent attacks from Taliban and al-Qaeda forces, most of which are based in neighboring Pakistan. However, experts say the insurgent forces are not a united, organized group but rather three or four factions, each with a different ideology and strategy, but united in their desire to force U.S. and other foreign forces out of Afghanistan.

In fact, close observers of Afghanistan say that when the Taliban government was toppled in 2001, it split into three groups. One group included mostly government bureaucrats and administrators; these Taliban surrendered and some joined the new government led by President Hamid Karzai. Another group was made up of the Taliban's senior leaders, including Mullah Omar, who fled across the border into Pakistan. The largest group of Taliban, however, were soldiers, local commanders, and provincial officials who simply returned to their farms and villages and remained in Afghanistan.

As security eroded in Afghanistan during the years following the 2001 U.S. invasion, various members of the Taliban began to reemerge. And Taliban leaders, now based in Pakistan, began contacting Taliban supporters who remained in Afghanistan. Many of these Taliban supporters are members of the Pashtun sect of Afghans who live in southern Afghanistan, whereas northern Afghanistan is home to other ethnic sects, such as the Tajiks and Hazaras. Over time, through intimidation, assassination, and promises of better security, this Pakistan-based group of Taliban has regained control of many parts of southern Afghanistan. In these rural villages, the Taliban recruit and pay fighters, settle disputes among villagers, and protect farmers' poppy fields—all actions that garner them support from many Afghan citizens. Some Taliban leaders also have modified some of their more extreme social rules; for example, senior leader Mullah Omar issued an edict allowing music and parties—activities that were banned when the Taliban controlled the government before 2001. This new version of the Taliban, now believed to be largely commanded by Mullah Brehadar, views itself as fighting on behalf of Afghans against a foreign occupation.

Another group of insurgents is composed of students and university-trained members of Hizb-i-Islami, a group led by warlord Gulbuddin Hekmatyar. During the 1980s, Hizb-i-Islami was one of the most extreme fundamentalist Islamic groups in the mujahideen fight against the Soviet occupation of Afghanistan. In fact, the United States provided the group with weapons and millions of dollars of aid during the Soviet-Afghan war. When the war ended, Hizb-i-Islami fought for power in Afghanistan's civil war, but once the Taliban won control of the country, Gulbuddin Hekmatyar fled to neighboring Iran. After the 2001 U.S. invasion, however, Hekmatyar returned to Afghanistan and reorganized Hizb-i-Islami, transforming it into one of the fastest growing insurgent groups in the country. While the Taliban is resurging in southern Afghanistan, Hizb-i-Islami forces are located near the capital city of Kabul and in northern provinces. Like the Taliban, the group seeks to expel foreign forces and reestablish an Islamic state in Afghanistan.

A third group of insurgents is led by Jalaluddin Haqqani, another former U.S. ally during the Soviet period, who once received millions of dollars and many high-tech missiles and weapons from the United States. Today, however, Haqqani is fighting U.S. forces in Afghanistan's eastern provinces. He is credited with bringing suicide bombing tactics to the Afghanistan war. Haqqani's group, according to observers, is more extreme than the Taliban and is closely tied to al-Qaeda. The group also is believed to be friendly with members of

Pakistan's intelligence forces, who have been linked to major attacks, including the July 2008 bombing of the Indian embassy in Kabul.

Yet a fourth group of insurgents is made up of Pakistani fighters from tribal areas in Pakistan near the Afghanistan border. Angered by U.S. attacks, this group agrees with many of the Taliban's strict Islamic rules, but remains independent of the Afghanistan Taliban. In 2007, experts say, this group of Pakistani Taliban formed a single group called the Tehrik-i-Taliban, led by a guerrilla fighter named Baitullah Mehsud. Pakistani officials believe Mehsud's group also is closely aligned with al-Qaeda and may have been involved in attacks in Pakistan, including the assassination of former Pakistani Prime Minister Benazir Bhutto. Today, a number of Tehrik-i-Taliban fighters focus on fighting Americans in Afghanistan.

Perhaps surprisingly, experts say al-Qaeda itself has largely stayed out of the Afghanistan insurgent movement. Al-Qaeda's message of global holy war, or *jihad*, is less important to many Afghans than personal security—the ability to live and be safe going about one's business. However, the mix of many different insurgent groups with ties to al-Qaeda, as well as connections to the Pakistan militants, makes the U.S. goal of bringing security to Afghanistan fraught with both military and political difficulties. The viewpoints in this chapter shed light on the complex situation in Afghanistan and offer an array of suggestions about ways to achieve the long-term goal of stabilizing the country.

Western Forces Need a Clear Strategy in Afghanistan

The Independent

The Independent *is a British newspaper.*

Barack Obama started to assume his responsibilities as president-elect with the lightest of sure touches last Friday. It is easy to see him as a modern Atlas, preparing to take the burdens of difficult global problems on his shoulders. As he answered reporters' questions with members of his transition team, however, he did not seem in the least cowed by the prospect. He spoke of the seriousness of the economic challenge that his administration will face when he assumes office on 20 January, but also dealt without any loss of dignity with the issue that obsessed most of those watching, including his daughters: the puppy.

The most pressing of the foreign policy burdens on his shoulders is, paradoxically, not Iraq but Afghanistan. His opposition to the invasion of Iraq was important in defining his position against those of George Bush, Hillary Clinton and John McCain, and in testifying to the quality of his judgement. But the issue declined in salience during the election campaign, partly because the government of Nouri al-Maliki in Baghdad gained in confidence and converged with the Obama line on early withdrawal. It may imply too much coherence to describe this as an exit strategy, but plainly the US engagement in Iraq is about to enter the winding-down phase.

In Afghanistan, on the other hand, the road ahead is less clear. This newspaper shares the view that president-elect Obama has expressed throughout his campaign: that the US-British coalition should reduce troop numbers in Iraq to focus on the war that is worth fighting in Afghanistan.

This is far from an easy option.

As Nick Clegg, the Liberal Democrat leader, is honest enough to argue below, this requires a surge in troop numbers in the short term. It will fall primarily to the US and Britain to provide those additional soldiers, given the failure of fellow NATO nations to come good on their promises to help rebuild Afghanistan.

The *Independent* on Sunday has never agreed with the crude anti-American argument that both Iraq and Afghanistan are wars of modern imperialism and that western troops should pull out come what may. The cause in Afghanistan was just and was indeed almost universally supported at the time in 2001 when the Taliban, harbourers of terrorists, were toppled. Since then, the international coalition has faced a choice: forget all about it and let the country slip back into warlordist theocracy, or think through what it would take to build a stable polity consistent with basic human rights—and do it.

As Mr Clegg points out, the worst option is to do nothing, because at the moment we have too few troops fighting an enemy that cannot be defeated by military means alone. Their task is, in the vivid phrase typical of the Army, that of "mowing the grass": once the Taliban are suppressed in one area and the international force moves on, they grow back.

If there were a clear political strategy leading to Afghans taking control of their own destiny, US, British and other NATO forces could ... support it.

So, more troops are needed, but we need a "civilian surge" too, to quote David Miliband, the Foreign Secretary. We need a political process—or, rather, a set of interlocking political processes—to render security objectives militarily achievable and sustainable. Put simply, the international forces in Afghanistan need to know what they are trying to achieve. As

Will Pike, an officer who served on the Afghanistan desk at the Ministry of Defence, says in our interview today: "No real thought is going into what we are doing and why."

We owe it to our armed forces to clarify these aims under the terms of the Military Covenant—the moral contract between the British people and their service personnel. Today of all days, as we remember those that have given their lives for their fellow citizens, we have to be straight with servicemen and women about our war aims.

That means building up the capability of the Kabul government's military forces; it means co-opting some of the more purely nationalist elements of the Taliban insurgency; and it means dealing with the sources of instability from outside the country, namely Pakistan and Iran. If there were a clear political strategy leading to Afghans taking control of their own destiny, US, British and other NATO forces could be asked with a clear conscience to support it.

In Afghanistan, as elsewhere in the world, we do not expect the impossible of president-elect Obama. Nothing can be guaranteed about the motives and tractability of the regimes in Iran, North Korea and Sudan, or, for example, of rebel leaders in the Congo. The least that can be said is that Mr Obama starts with a clean slate. But his emphasis on dialogue, his focus on a war worth fighting—rather than one that the world thinks was a mistake—and his thoughtfulness suggest that, if all the rough places are not made plain, then at least the prospects for the world are better than they were before.

The United States Must Provide Enough Troops and Resources to Win a Long War in Afghanistan

Anthony Cordesman

Anthony Cordesman is an author, an expert on national security and the Middle East, and a fellow at the Center for Strategic and International Studies, a public policy research institution.

We need to recognize just how grim the realities have become in the Afghan-Pakistan conflict. As recent reports by *ABC* and the *New York Times* show, US intelligence has produced a NIE [National Intelligence Estimate] stating that we face a steadily stronger enemy that is winning in the ways that count. Taliban [a fundamentalist Islamic militia] [Gulbuddin] Hekmatyar [a former rebel commander during the Soviet-Afghan war] and [Jalaluddin] Haqqani [an Afghan military leader] influence have steadily expanded in both Afghanistan, and FATA [Federally Administered Tribal Areas] and Baluchi areas of Pakistan since 2004. Similar reports show that the White House has finally recognized that we have failed to provide the troops, aid personnel, and money necessary to win the war, and have been forced to try to totally rethink the strategies that have now failed for more than half a decade.

The US, NATO/ISAF [North Atlantic Treaty Organization/ International Security Assistance Force, a group of countries providing security to Afghanistan], and Afghan government may still win tactical clashes, as may the Pakistan Army and Frontier Corps, but this is not the real war. The real war is political, ideological, and a struggle for the control of political and economic space. It is also a war of political attrition.

Anthony Cordesman, *Winning the War in Afghanistan: The Realities of 2009*. Washington, D.C.: Center for Strategic & International Studies, 2008. Reproduced by permission.

The Taliban and its allies win if they simply outlast NATO/ ISAF and the US, and force the Afghan and Pakistani governments in ways that make them part of the government or give them de facto control of territory.

An End to Spin and False Optimism

We cannot win through false optimism, by exploring creative proposals that take years to implement, or by trying to substitute reorganization for resources. We cannot win by not providing meaningful reporting and transparency on what is actually happening. We cannot win by refusing to report on the military situation, even to the extent that we report on Iraq. We cannot win by never really discussing the resources being provided. We cannot win by not reporting on the problems in developing effective Afghan security forces and governance. We cannot win by never accounting for where the money we spend actually goes, and never reporting on meaningful measures of effectiveness for military and civil aid expenditures.

We cannot win [the Afghan war] unless we provide the proper resources, honest measures of effectiveness, and honest timelines for success.

We are running out of time. There will not be any single moment of crisis in the Afghan-Pakistan War, but we cannot afford to go through another year in which we fail to deploy key capabilities, giving the enemy the initiative. . . .

As a recent CSIS [Center for Strategic and International Studies, a think tank] study shows, the [George W.] Bush Administration . . . failed for more than half a decade to deploy the necessary resources in the field and the people necessary to use them. It has tried to export the problem to a weak and corrupt Afghan government that will take years to fix, or to NATO allies recruited for a peacekeeping mission that has turned into a real war. It has spent some 20% of the money and provided 20% of forces for Afghanistan that it has spent on Iraq, although the wars are of roughly the same scale.

Under the best of circumstances, "winning" the Afghan-Pakistan War will be relative. Only the Afghans and Pakistanis can ultimately provide the combination of improved governance, economics, rule of law, and ideological counters to Islamist extremism necessary to produce secure and stable countries. Creating the security and stability to make this possible, however, requires the US to accept a series of unpleasant facts and act upon them immediately:

- We currently are losing, and the trends have been consistent since 2004.

- We cannot win unless we provide the proper resources, honest measures of effectiveness, and honest timelines for success.

- Almost all of the necessary added resources will come from us. They will not come from our allies, by creating an effective central government in Afghanistan, or by US efforts to pressure or win support in Pakistan. The problems with NATO/ISAF, [Afghanistan President Hamid] Karzai, and Pakistan are known quantities where improvement may be possible to some degree, but this war will be won or lost by US resources and actions.

- Exporting problems and responsibility to others will ensure that we lose, and often produces a serious backlash in terms of Afghan, Pakistani, and allied reactions. Trying to win a "blame game" with Karzai, NATO, and Pakistan will do more to alienate than persuade, and cost more than it will gain.

- We need to stop the spin and liar's contests, and provide honest public reporting. We need enough transparency and credibility to get sustained Congressional,

Media, and public support for a long war. This means Afghan reporting needs at least the same level of honesty and detail now found in the Department of Defense quarterly reports on security and stability in Iraq, the State Department weekly status report on Iraq, and the Quarterly reports of the Special Inspector General for Iraqi Reconstruction. It also means providing unclassified summaries of key intelligence reports like the new NIE on Afghanistan, rather than delaying the completion of even the classified version because a leak might affect the election.

We face a crisis in the field—right now. "Winning" . . . [requires] sorting out the flood of existing ideas to see what can actually be done in the field in 2009 and 2010.

We Need Effective Leadership, Planning, Resources, and Execution

We have a flood of ideas, concepts, Powerpoint oversimplifications, and supposed "strategies." In practice, most of them range from well-meaning nonsense to rearranging the deck chairs on the Titanic.

Yes, it would help to reorganize the fractured US/NATO/ISAF command structure. It would help to try to ease national caveats, to speed improvements in Afghan governance, to find better negotiating forums to bring together Afghanistan and Pakistan. There is also much that the US and the world could do to improve their mid- and long-term efforts at aid and nation building in Afghanistan and Pakistan if the war and security situation can be improved over the next few years.

But, we face a crisis in the field—right now. "Winning" does not require new ideas as much as sorting out the flood of existing ideas to see what can actually be done in the field in 2009 and 2010.

This requires detailed and workable plans to fight the war we now face and to win in the field at the local level. It requires net assessments of the current situation and detailed priorities for action. It requires equally detailed plans for tangible action with clear timelines. It requires budgets, deployment schedules, and clear statements of the necessary resources and where we will get them.

Moreover, we need to understand that endless meetings and discussion sessions in Washington, Brussels, Mons and other locations far from the actual country team in Afghanistan and Pakistan can only talk the situation into defeat. Proper preparation must come through the US ambassador and commander in the field, but they can only act if they have the troops, aid personnel, and dollars to turn preparation and opportunity into success. Any form of "clear, hold, and build" that works at the local level will be a matter of local adaptation that actually succeeds in the field. It also requires concerted local action and resources at the national, provincial, and district level in 2009 and 2010.

- We need to stop talking about strategy in a generic sense that does not go beyond ideas, that does not require serious resources, and that does not honestly address real-world organization, command, interagency, and coordination problems. A better strategy—clearly linked to detailed plans, time lines, and resources can help, but slogans, concepts, and ideas are not a strategy. A strategy must include detailed force plans, aid plans, resource plans, measures of effectiveness and audits.

- At least for the near term, we need a "resource push" to compensate for years of underreacting, and dodging unpleasant issues and truths. We need assets in 2009 and 2010, not plans. The lead times on getting new troops, aid personnel and efforts, and more effective Afghan and Pakistani security forces into the field next year are already daunting.

- We cannot bypass NATO, the Afghan central government, or the Pakistani central government, but we also cannot rely on victory by committee. We need a clear central US point in charge of US efforts in the entire war that cut across allied interagency, command, and country team issues. We also need to coordinate intelligence, net assessment, and resource management to match. The best place to do this is almost certainly CENTCOM [U.S. Central Command], backed by stronger country teams, and more US troops, advisors, and aid personnel in the field.

- We do, however, need to shape our efforts in ways that recognize that we have both mid- and long-term objectives. We need a quick fix that has to be resource driven for now, but we also need to stop looking for quick and simple solutions to the overall challenge of the war and nation building. Even if we can decisively reverse the enemy's momentum in 2009–2010, we are talking about a long war that will last through [at] least the next presidency—assuming the new president is reelected. There are reasons that some of the Powerpoints developed by the US command in Afghanistan show time lines through 2019.

The United States Should Halt All Military Operations in Afghanistan

Sameer Dossani

Sameer Dossani is the director of 50 Years Is Enough: U.S. Network for Global Economic Justice, a coalition of more than 200 U.S. organizations dedicated to the transformation of the World Bank and the International Monetary Fund (IMF).

In recent history, two concepts of justice have stood out. Dr. Martin Luther King, Jr., believed in a kind of justice that could only be achieved when systematic oppression had been eliminated from the world. Along the way, people would have to be held accountable for their crimes. Those who had done wrong would have to admit that they had done wrong and pay some appropriate restitution for their crimes, as happened decades later in South Africa's truth and reconciliation commissions. But justice was forever intertwined with a changing of the human spirit for Dr. King. It was the societal uplifting of love over hate, of human dignity over human debasement. It was a coming to terms with our violent history and affirming values of love and compassion over those of hate and retribution.

[Former U.S. president] George W. Bush, on the other hand, believed in the justice of old Western movies and gunfights. . . .

[President] Barack Obama will have to choose between these two approaches. The decision he makes will reverberate around the world and be one of the first indicators of whether "Change We Can Believe In" was merely good sloganeering.

Ending Bush's imperial misadventures in Iraq will certainly be a top priority for the incoming administration, but Obama will also be tested in Afghanistan. His words so far—calling Afghanistan the "central front" in the "War on Terror" and demanding more military action against insurgents allied with the Taliban—don't inspire confidence that he would choose the King doctrine over the Bush doctrine.

The [2001] invasion ... brought down a terrible fundamentalist regime while taking an inordinately heavy toll in civilian casualties.

Reckless Interventions

In 1996, the Taliban, a faction of the anti-Soviet Mujahideen [rebels who fought the Soviet occupation of Afghanistan] with fundamentalist Wahabi Muslim beliefs, took control of Kabul [Afghanistan's capital] and most of Afghanistan. Zbigniew Brzezinski, [former U.S. president] Jimmy Carter's National Security Advisor, supported the Mujahideen (who from the very beginning had fundamentalist tendencies) as part of the "Afghan trap" which succeeded in fatally wounding the Soviet empire. While many Afghans greeted the Taliban's rise to power with delight, their theocratic government soon began to grate on the people of Afghanistan, for whom fundamentalist Islam was almost as foreign as Mormonism.

After the events of September 11, 2001, the Bush administration portrayed the Taliban as deeply connected with al-Qaeda, the terrorist network that claimed responsibility for the attacks, and therefore argued for going to war against Afghanistan. When the Taliban countered that they were happy to give up Osama bin Laden, the alleged mastermind of the 9/11 attacks, if the U.S. could produce any evidence for the allegation, the U.S. scoffed. Then the U.S. invaded.

The invasion succeeded in two things: First, it brought down a terrible fundamentalist regime while taking an inordinately heavy toll in civilian causalities. The Taliban had instituted a brutal form of *shariah* law [Islamic religious law] and forced minorities to wear identification tags. They had even destroyed ancient Buddhist carvings claiming that the depiction of the human form is "unislamic." Many Afghans—particularly the half of the population who happen to be women—were excited to see the Taliban ousted. While this is an accomplishment, it's worth remembering that expectations for improvement in women's lives were largely unmet.

The second and even more dangerous accomplishment of the U.S. invasion of Afghanistan was to elevate the Taliban, al-Qaeda and anyone willing to resist U.S. aggression to the status of heroes or freedom fighters.

Perhaps the easiest way to understand what most Afghans and many South Asians, Muslims, and others around the world felt after the invasion is to remember how Americans felt after the September 11 attacks. George W. Bush was a deeply unpopular president. The election that brought him to power had split the population, with shady dealings in Florida and an activist Supreme Court ultimately deciding the race in favor of Bush. Many of my liberal compatriots despised the president, who was already acquiring a reputation for spending his presidency on vacation.

The United Nations charter gives the Taliban and other Afghans the right to legitimate self-defense against U.S. aggression.

But after the 9/11 attacks, those same liberals were rallying around Bush. The logic was simple: in a time of crisis, with your country under attack, you support those who are going to defend you. You may not like George W. Bush, but his policies [and] his armed forces stand between you and whoever caused significant damage to New York and Washington, DC.

By the same logic, who stood between Afghan civilians and the NATO [North Atlantic Treaty Organization, an alliance of European and North American countries] aerial bombardments that killed about 3,000 people? The Taliban. Every bomb that detonated on a wedding party led to tens, perhaps hundreds of young people—mostly young boys and many of them orphans—joining the resistance movement under the flag of the Taliban.

And it's not just that the Afghan population *believes* that the Taliban resistance is legitimate; that resistance *is* legitimate under international law. No less important a document than the United Nations charter gives the Taliban and other Afghans the right to legitimate self-defense against U.S. aggression.

The Real War Against Fundamentalism

So if aerial bombardments and occupations give legitimacy to those very fundamentalists who Afghans would remove from power, what does the real war on fundamentalism look like? In 1999 I was the first staff person of the International Network for the Rights of Female Victims of Violence in Pakistan, a group that was combating "honor crimes" along the Pakistan-Afghanistan border. These were incidences of domestic violence, often against a wife, a sister, a daughter or even a mother who was accused of having some kind of illicit sexual relationship. We understood that these crimes were on the rise because of the spread of Taliban-style Wahabi Islam into tribal areas that already had an extremely patriarchal view of women's bodies.

What was our weapon of choice in fighting against the Talibanization of what has traditionally been a tolerant, ecumenical form of Islam? Education. We taught women their rights under Pakistani and Afghani law, we taught about the passages in the Quran that mentioned women's rights, and we also tried to educate people about other traditions—whether they be secular humanist traditions or the Hindu and Christian traditions of neighboring countries and tribes. In other words we tried to undermine the hatred, the xenophobia, the fear upon which fundamentalism is built.

Such efforts may take generations, and they almost always require the state to play a role in education, development and ensuring employment for all. But ultimately education is the only way to combat religious fundamentalism, just as negotiation is ultimately the only way to end war.

Buying into a Failed Solution

While Obama's election may indicate a shift in U.S. foreign policy (and hopefully a rejection of the Bush doctrine of preemptive war), Obama has prescribed more military operations in Afghanistan.

For more than a year, Obama has argued for redeploying U.S. troops from Iraq to Afghanistan. He has called Afghanistan the "central front in the War on Terror" and has even threatened to bomb Pakistan should there be evidence that Afghan warlords are hiding there and the Pakistani government isn't "doing enough" about it. (On this last point, Bush has already bombed Pakistan several times over the last few months, prompting the Pakistani government to publicly rebuke the U.S. for violating its sovereignty.)

Instead of scaling up an already disastrous war, the United States could change course . . . [by] withdrawing troops.

While Obama's rhetoric in arguing for increased involvement in Afghanistan makes some sense—he claims that Bush has been so involved with Iraq that the al-Qaeda leaders who allegedly orchestrated the September 11 attacks are still at large—his proposed methodology doesn't.

Instead of scaling up an already disastrous war, the United States could change course in a way that would ultimately do a lot more to ensure the world's safety. Such measures should include:

1. Withdrawing troops. International law is clear on this subject. No country may occupy another indefinitely and certainly not without the will of the people being occupied. If an Obama administration truly thinks that withdrawing U.S. and NATO troops would be a bad thing for Afghans, hold a referendum to see who would like the troops to remain.

2. Working with the various Afghan factions to begin negotiations. Wars are rarely stopped on the battlefield, and those that are have a tendency to break out again after a few years. The recent history of Afghanistan illustrates this point. It's better by far for enemies and friends, Pashtun, Tajik, and others to settle differences through negotiation based on mutual respect and the rule of law.

3. Once stability and security are guaranteed in Afghanistan, beginning the attack on fundamentalism in earnest. Working to incorporate Afghanistan into the international human rights framework through enforcing UN [United Nations] measures which Afghanistan has already ratified, such as the Convention on the Elimination of All Forms of Discrimination against Women is one step that can be taken in this regard. Another is major investment in social infrastructure and particularly health and education measures which will ultimately help Afghanistan recover from being bombed "into the stone age."

If the idea of immediately stopping all military operations in Afghanistan sounds radical, it shouldn't. No less than President Hamid Karzai pleaded for an end to the bombings immediately after the U.S. election, as yet another wedding party fell victim to bombs from the sky.

For the sake of all [of] us, Afghan and American, let's hope President Barack Obama heeds his call.

Good Government Is What Afghanistan Most Desperately Needs

Sarah Chayes

Sarah Chayes is a journalist and the author of The Punishment of Virtue: Inside Afghanistan After the Taliban *(2006). She also runs an Afghan cooperative that produces skin-care products.*

Nurallah strode into our workshop shaking with rage. His mood shattered ours. "This is no government," he stormed. "The police are like animals."

The story gushed out of him: There'd been a fender-bender in the Kandahar bazaar, a taxi and a bicycle among wooden-wheeled vegetable carts. Wrenching around to avoid the knot, another cart touched one of the green open-backed trucks the police drive. In seconds, the officers were dragging the man to the chalky dust, beating him—blow after blow to the head, neck, hips, kidneys. Shopkeepers in the nearby stalls began shouting, "What do you want to do, kill him?" The police slung the man into the back of their truck and roared away.

"So he made a mistake," concluded Nurallah, one of the 13 Afghan men and women who make up my cooperative. "We don't have a traffic court? They had to beat him?"

In the seven years I've lived in this stronghold of the Afghan south—the erstwhile capital of the Taliban and the focus of their renewed assault on the country—most of my conversations with locals about what's going wrong have centered on corruption and abuse of power. "More than roads, more than schools or wells or electricity, we need good governance," said Nurallah during yet another discussion a couple of weeks ago.

He had put his finger on the heart of the problem. We and our friends in Kandahar are thunderstruck at recent suggestions that the solution to the hair-raising situation in this country must include a political settlement with "relevant parties"—read, the Taliban. Negotiating with them wouldn't solve Afghanistan's problems; it would only exacerbate them. Ask any Afghan what's really needed, what would render the Taliban irrelevant, and they'll tell you: improving the behavior of the officials whom the United States and its allies ushered into power after the Sept. 11, 2001, terrorist attacks.

Ask any Afghan what's really needed, what would render the Taliban irrelevant, and they'll tell you: improving the behavior of the [government] officials.

I write this by flickering light, a fat candle at my right elbow and a kerosene lamp on my left. We get only three or four hours of electricity every couple of days, often from 1 to 5 a.m. Still, the bill has to be paid. To do that, you must wait in a total of eight lines in two different buildings. You almost never get through the whole process without hearing an uncouth bark as your turn comes up: "This desk is closing; come back tomorrow." Due to the electricity shortage, the power department won't open new accounts. Officially. But for $600—15 times the normal fee and a fortune to Afghans—you can get a meter installed anyway.

A friend recently visited the jail in Urozgan Province, north of Kandahar, where he found 54 prisoners. All but six were untried and uncharged and had been languishing there for months or years. A Kandahar public prosecutor told him how a defendant had once offered him the key to a Lexus if he would just refrain from interfering in a case the man had fixed.

Across the street from my cooperative there used to be a medical clinic. When it moved to a new facility, gunmen in police uniforms set up a checkpoint outside the empty building. Our inquiries revealed that they were the private guards of a senior government official. Their purpose? To serve as a graphic warning to the building's owners not to interfere in what would follow. A few days later, some friends of the official's moved in. The owners had no say in the matter, no recourse. This government official is one of the men the United States helped put in power in 2001 and whom the international community has maintained and supported, no questions asked, ever since.

Since [2001] . . . , the hopes expressed by every Afghan I have encountered—to be ruled by a responsive and respectful government run by educated people—have been dashed.

This is why the Taliban are making headway in Afghanistan—not because anyone loves them, even here in their former heartland, or longs for a return to their punishing rule. I arrived in Kandahar in December 2001, just days after Taliban leader Mullah Muhammad Omar was chased out. After a moment of holding its breath, the city erupted in joy. Kites danced on the air for the first time in six years. Buyers flocked to stalls selling music cassettes. I listened to opium dealers discuss which of them would donate the roof of his house for use as a neighborhood school. I, a barefaced American woman, encountered no hostility at all. Curiosity, plenty. But no hostility. Enthusiasm for the nascent government of Hamid Karzai and its international backers was absolutely universal.

Since then, the hopes expressed by every Afghan I have encountered—to be ruled by a responsive and respectful government run by educated people—have been dashed. Now, Afghans are suffering so acutely that they hardly feel the difference between Taliban depredations and those of their own government. "We're like a man trying to stand on two water-melons," one of the women in my cooperative complains. "The Taliban shake us down at night, and the government shakes us down in the daytime."

I hear from Westerners that corruption is intrinsic to Afghan culture, that we should not hold Afghans up to our standards. I hear that Afghanistan is a tribal place, that it has never been, and can't be, governed.

But that's not what I hear from Afghans.

Afghans looked to the United States—a nation famous for its rule of law—to help them build a responsive, accountable government.

Afghans remember the reign in the 1960s and '70s of King Zahir Shah and his cousin Daoud Khan, when Afghan cities were among the most developed and cosmopolitan in the Muslim world, when Peace Corps volunteers conducted vaccination campaigns on foot through a welcoming countryside, and when, my friends here tell me, a lone, unarmed policeman could detain a criminal suspect in a far-flung village without obstruction. Kandaharis—even those who lost a brother or father in the 1980s war against Soviet occupation—praise the communist-backed government of former president Najibullah. "His officials weren't building marble-clad mansions with the money they extorted," says Fayzullah, another member of my cooperative.

One day I asked three of my colleagues—villagers with almost no formal education—what jobs they would choose if we were the municipal government of Kandahar. They spoke right up. "I would want to be in charge of public hygiene," said Karim. "The garbage piling up on our streets is a disgusting health hazard." Abd al-Ahad wanted to be the registrar of public deeds, "so the big people can't just take land and pass it out to their cronies." Nurallah wanted to be the equivalent of the FDA: the man responsible for weights and measures and the quality of merchandise in the bazaar.

After the Soviet invasion, which cost a million Afghan lives over the course of the 1980s, followed by five years of gut-wrenching civil war and another six of rule by the Taliban, who twisted religious injunctions into instruments of social control, Afghans looked to the United States—a nation famous for its rule of law—to help them build a responsive, accountable government.

Instead, we gave power back to corrupt gunslingers who had been repudiated years before. If they helped us chase al-Qaeda, we didn't look too hard at their governing style. Often we helped them monopolize the new opportunities for gain. A friend of mine, one of the beneficiaries, was astounded at the blank check. "What are we warlords doing still in power?" police precinct captain Mahmad Anwar asked me in 2002. "I vowed on the Holy Koran that I would fight the Taliban in order to bring an educated, competent government to Afghanistan. And now people like me are running the place?" I had to laugh at his candor.

Into the context of the white-hot frustration that has been building since then, insert the Taliban. Since 2001, they have been armed, financed, trained and coordinated in Pakistan, whose military intelligence agency—the ISI—first helped create them in 1994.

What I've witnessed in Kandahar since late 2002 has amounted to an invasion by proxy, with the Pakistani military once again using the Taliban to gain a foothold in Afghanistan. The only reason this invasion has made progress is the appalling behavior of Afghan officials. Why would anyone defend officials who pillage them? If the Taliban gouge out the eyes of people they accuse of colluding with the Afghan government, as they did recently in Kandahar, while the government treats those same citizens like rubbish, why should anyone take the risk that allegiance to Kabul entails?

More and more Kandaharis are not. More and more are severing contact with the Karzai regime and all it stands for, rejecting even development assistance. When Taliban thugs come to their mosques demanding money or food, they pay up. Many actively collaborate, as a means of protest.

The solution is to call to account the officials we installed [in Afghanistan] . . . in 2001—to reach . . . ordinary Afghan citizens and give their grievances a fair hearing.

The solution to this problem is not to bring the perpetrators of the daily horrors we suffer in Kandahar to the table to carve up the Afghan pie. (For no matter how we package the idea of negotiating with the Taliban, that's what Afghans are sure it will amount to: cutting a power-sharing deal.)

The solution is to call to account the officials we installed here beginning in 2001—to reach beyond the power brokers to ordinary Afghan citizens and give their grievances a fair hearing. If the complaints prove to be well founded, Western officials should press for redress, using some of their enormous leverage. The successful mentoring program under which military personnel work side-by-side with Afghan National Army officers should be expanded to the civilian administration. Western governments should send experienced former mayors, district commissioners and water and health department officials to mentor Afghans in those roles.

If the United States and its allies had fulfilled their initial promise and pushed the Afghan government to become an institution its people could be proud of, the "reconcilable" Taliban would come into the fold of their own accord. The Afghans would take care of the rest.

More International Investment Will Bring Security to Afghanistan

Greg Bruno with Mahmoud Saikal

Greg Bruno is a staff writer for the Council on Foreign Relations, a non-partisan membership organization that seeks to promote understanding of foreign policy and America's role in the world. Mahmoud Saikal is Afghanistan's former deputy foreign minister and senior advisor on the Afghanistan National Development Strategy.

When Hamid Karzai greets donors in Paris on June 12, the Afghan president will officially unveil Afghanistan's first national development strategy. A focal point of the package is its price tag—$50 billion—a hefty sum for a country with a tenuous record managing its own redevelopment effort. But Mahmoud Saikal, Afghanistan's former deputy foreign minister and an adviser on the national strategy, says the international community must look past concerns about corruption and insecurity and invest in his country's future. "If we invest more in Afghanistan, chances are we will bring security," he says. "The two go hand in hand." Saikal says the national development strategy, two years in the making, will serve as Afghanistan's blueprint to guide itself from decades of war and conflict.

[Greg Bruno:] Let's start with a brief outline of the Afghan National Development Strategy. Help us understand what this document is and why it's needed.

[Mahmoud Saikal:] The Afghanistan National Development Strategy [ANDS] is the medium-term development strategy for Afghanistan. It also serves as a poverty reduction strategy paper which has been proposed to the World Bank and the IMF [International Monetary Fund]. It has been prepared by using the PRSP, or Poverty Reduction Strategy Paper method-ology, which means that it had to have a poverty focus, sound macrofinance work, sector policies, a consultative process and so on. The ANDS is Afghanistan's overarching strategy for promoting growth, generating wealth, and reducing poverty and vulnerability in general.

Why is it needed?

In late 2001, when the Bonn Agreement [on the makeup of a post-Taliban government] was signed by various parties, it chalked out a political strategy for putting things together for the next few years. By the end of 2005, the benchmark of the Bonn Agreement was coming to an end and the Afghans, as well as the world community, wanted to know what to do next. This is why there was a need inside Afghanistan and also a need for the international community to know what to do in the next few years. This is why, when the London Confer-ence took place in January 2006, two key documents emerged from that conference. One was the Afghanistan Compact and the other one was a version of the Afghanistan National De-velopment Strategy. Now the strategy in a way was a blueprint for the development of Afghanistan but with a particular fo-cus on three key pillars. Pillar one was security, pillar two was governance and rule of law and human rights, and pillar three was development and economic issues.

The Afghanistan National Development Strategy [ANDS] is the medium-term development strategy for Afghani-stan.

Among the questions that have surfaced in advance of the Paris conference is the price tag for the strategy: $50 billion. Why is so *much money needed and what makes Afghanistan think that the international community is prepared to spend that much on Afghanistan's redevelopment?*

Number one, with the passage of time now we know the scale of the conflict in Afghanistan. Now we know the kind of damage Afghanistan has seen—over thirty years of war and conflict. At the beginning, seven years ago, we had no idea. We didn't have facts and figures and all those things. This is why when we went to the Tokyo Conference, which was the first donor conference in January 2002, we had no idea of the scale of devastation. So that's one reason. Number two: We are putting up a strategy for the next five years, so it's a sort of medium-term strategy, which needs a large amount of money. But the way it is, the breakdown of the $50 billion, [is such] that $24 billion of that has already been pledged in the past and we anticipate another $6 or $7 billion coming from our own revenues. So, all together it has to be something a little bit less than $20 billion that we would be asking for. And so far, in the discussion that we've had with the donor community, we're confident that at least a very good percentage of what we are asking for will be covered in Paris.

The Afghan government has sought more control of donor dollars, a request some in the international community have resisted. Donors contend they haven't seen evidence Afghanistan is ready to control funds, and they often cite corruption as one of the reasons. What assurances can the Afghan government give to donors that corruption won't undermine the assistance?

With the passage of time now we know the scale of the conflict in Afghanistan . . . over thirty years of war and conflict.

Under the ANDS the capacity building and fighting corruption and so on has been given top priority. So what happens in every sector, capacity building and being able to deliver the goods, has been given priority. A good percentage of international aid will go toward confidence building, will go toward transparency, will go toward capacity building of Afghan institutions. We can only fight corruption if there is international support; we can only establish transparency if there is international support. Let's not forget that building that quality governance takes time. Quality governance needs quality human resources and quality human resources need having a mechanism through which we could allow our quality human resources to come to governance, and these are the kind of things that we are doing.

In real fact, we've been busy building up government administration only for the past three or four years. Before that it was an emergency situation and it was a transition period. Two, three, or four years in the life of building up a government is not much. Building government bureaucracy takes time.

The World Bank recently reviewed the ANDS and suggested that it suffers from a lack of prioritization of key development programs. Is such criticism valid?

Two, three, or four years in the life of building up a government is not much. Building government bureaucracy takes time.

Afghanistan has been hit from every angle for thirty-odd years and it's been badly damaged. So it is very, very difficult to develop black and white lists of priorities because the fact is we have to be mobilized in different fields simultaneously—and we have to work simultaneously. Security needs development; development needs security. You know, agriculture, for example. Now as we get into Paris, at the top of our list there are a few things which include irrigation, agriculture, energy, followed by health, education and so on. But really, we've had some achievement in the past in the field of infrastructure, namely transportation, for example. We have been successful in putting the Afghanistan national ring road together. Up until today we've finished about 70 percent of that. We have been successful, for example, in the field of communication. Nowadays, four and a half billion Afghans have access to mobile telephones. But we are lagging behind in some other sectors now, after seven years, in particular, agriculture and irrigation. And this is why when we go to Paris the emphasis shall remain on irrigation, agriculture, and energy.

The strategy places a very heavy reliance on the idea of privatization luring international and domestic partners to invest money. But the strategy acknowledges that to do that security needs to first be achieved. How does the ANDS address the continuing needs of security in the provinces?

To start with, if you're an investor and want to invest, no matter where you are, whether you are in the United States or Afghanistan or in Europe, there are risks of different kinds that you have to accept. I don't think you can find anywhere in the world where there is risk-free investment. The only trouble is that in Afghanistan the risk could be higher. But at the same time, those investors who have taken risks in the past seven years—they have been making profit. Take the example of the telecommunications sector. So far we've got four companies who have licenses in Afghanistan. Two of them moved into Afghanistan at a time when we had no idea what the future was going to be like. But now they're here, and they're making profit [Afghan Wireless, owned by an Afghan businessman, was formed in 2002; its competitor, Roshan, began operating in 2003]. Recently we saw the tendering of the copper mine of Aynak in Logar Province of Afghanistan, [where] a very big Chinese company moved in.

Security needs development and development needs security. If we invest more in Afghanistan, chances are that we will bring security. But if we stay away from Afghanistan, chances are Afghanistan will see more insecurity. So, you know, the two go hand in hand.

The ANDS talks about the 'Afghanization' of redevelopment. How important is it for the Afghan government and the Afghan people to feel ownership over this redevelopment strategy?

The call for international aid to be channeled to Afghan institutions is timely. That is another move toward Afghanization. But the terminology of Afghanization came into being when we were discussing security. About a year and a half ago there was a strong call by the Afghans and the international community that the time had come that we Afghanized the security of the country. We support the security agencies, mainly defense, the Afghanistan National Army, the police force, and the National Security Directorate. The focus was on security but now we are moving it into the other sectors, making sure that Afghans take control, but of course with the backing and with the support of the international community.

If we invest more in Afghanistan, chances are that we will bring security. But if we stay away from Afghanistan, chances are Afghanistan will see more insecurity.

So the message in Paris will be a nuanced one. On one hand Afghanistan is ready to take the reins but on the other Afghanistan can't do it alone.

Of course. The point is that two-and-a-half years ago when we went to the London Conference there was a pledge in there. The pledge was that the Afghans would put a national development strategy together and the international community would support that strategy and make sure that the implementation of that strategy would take place smoothly. That meant that the international community would extend technical support and financial support to the implementation of this strategy. Now, two and a half years on, we're going to Paris and we let the world know that now we have this strategy ready. The time has come that we reconfirm the political support of the international community and also the technical and financial support of the international community toward the implementation of the national development strategy.

The United States Must Control the Taliban's Drug Trade

Robert I. Rotberg

Robert I. Rotberg is director of the Program on Intrastate Conflict at Harvard's Kennedy School of Government, and he is president of the World Peace Foundation, a foundation that seeks to advance the cause of peace through study, analysis, and advocacy.

The United States and NATO [North Atlantic Treaty Organization, an alliance of European and North American countries] are about to lose the war in Afghanistan to an insurgent, revived Taliban [a fundamentalist Islamic militia]. Deprived of sufficient firepower and soldiers, Allied forces are failing to hunt down and contain the Taliban, especially in the southern part of the country. Moreover, the crucial battle for Pashtun [an ethnic tribe accounting for a little more than half the Afghan population] hearts and minds is also about to be lost. Only the rapid provision of security, roads, electricity, and educational and health services can counter the appeal of the renewed and reinvigorated Taliban. Urgently required are more troops for security and more funds for rebuilding essential services.

Attacking the Drug Trade

Narco-trafficking is fueling the Taliban, and fat profits from poppies and opium are partially responsible for the militants' resurgence. Indeed, Afghanistan is supplying about 90 percent of the world's opium and nearly all of the heroin that ends up in Europe. A recent study by the UN [United Nations] Office

Robert I. Rotberg, "Losing the War in Afghanistan," *The Boston Globe*, April 2, 2007. Reproduced by permission of the author.

for Drugs and Crime forecasts a record crop of poppies this year [2007], on top of last year's bumper harvest.

To undercut the ability of the Taliban to purchase arms, pay soldiers, and buy the support of villagers, the United States and NATO need to break the back of the drug trade in and out of Afghanistan. However, reliance on eradication—the current weapon of choice—is foolish and wasteful. Uprooting crops and spraying have both had limited local effect. What is needed is a radically new, incentive-based method to provide better incomes to farmers from substitute crops.

What is needed is a radically new, incentive-based method to provide better incomes to farmers from substitute crops.

Many Afghan officials have urged farmers to grow saffron or almonds instead of poppies. But the only viable substitute crop is wheat, an Afghan staple. Sometimes it is in short supply, too. If the West would guarantee above-market prices for wheat over 10 years, and establish a transparent method to buy unlimited quantities of wheat from Afghan farmers through an official marketing system, it is likely that Afghan farmers would gradually switch from poppies to wheat. And they could eat any wheat that becomes surplus. Furthermore, guaranteeing a high price for wheat would probably cost less than the billions devoted to eradication. It would also put more money than from poppies directly into the pockets of farmers and, simultaneously, cut out middlemen and traffickers.

Inventing such a scheme is the only way to undercut the appeal of the Taliban. Extirpating its troops by conventional military means will remain impossible without curtailing the flow of men and material from Taliban support bases in Pakistan. It is not yet clear that the Pakistani intelligence services are ready to cripple the Taliban in that way. NATO has too few troops and too little good intelligence to do so itself without Pakistan's help or without limitations on the Taliban's supply of cash through narcotics.

Winning the Trust of the Afghan People

In many civil wars, winning the trust and cooperation of the beleaguered civil population is essential. In Afghanistan the American-backed government of President Hamid Karzai has much too little progress to report. Seventy percent of all Afghan businesses still run generators so they can operate for a few hours a day. There is little centrally generated electricity, potable water is scarce, the road network is still potholed and poor, jobs are scarce, educational opportunity remains limited, and health facilities are spartan. Most of all, the countryside and the cities are increasingly insecure.

It is true that credible elections have been held and that parliament, representing the entire country, has often curtailed the power of the executive. It is true that parts of Kabul are booming, thanks to international activity. It is also true that sections of northern Afghanistan are peaceful, and responding well to the earnest efforts of NATO missions.

But the more populous, Pashtun-dominated south is more and more at war. That is the consuming challenge for NATO and American forces. Those forces need to show that they can stifle the narcotics trade, prevent Talibani movement across the Pakistani border, and oust the Taliban from strongholds in southern provinces. Most of all, they must begin to win the trust and cooperation of citizens through lasting good works and by showing that NATO forces are in the south to stay. No Afghan believes that they are.

Winning in Afghanistan is a tall order. It will rely on major Afghan government and donor support, a concerted battle over drugs, and a clear demonstration to Afghan villagers that NATO will win. Otherwise, the Taliban will play upon people's fears and gain strength in a clash of wills with a weakened NATO.

The United States Must Grow the Afghan Army

Robert D. Kaplan

Robert D. Kaplan is a foreign correspondent for The Atlantic, *an American magazine that focuses on foreign affairs, politics, the economy, and cultural trends.*

Presidient ... Barack Obama has said that he wants to focus attention on Afghanistan, which, as opposed to Iraq, represents the legitimate War on Terrorism. In fact, the real situation is slightly different. The United States economy is in such bad shape that domestic issues will have to be his primary concern, meaning he needs Iraq to stay off the front pages and Afghanistan to start showing some amelioration [improvement] so that he can busy himself with issues like reducing unemployment and lifting the U.S. out of recession.

How does he do this?

He's already made a good start in Iraq. By appointing centrist pragmatists like Marine Gen. (Ret.) James Jones and Sen. Hillary Clinton to top national security positions, and reappointing Defense Secretary Robert Gates, he has sent a message in the face of an uptick in violence in Iraq that his administration will not be rushing for the exits there, so as not to risk a disintegration of the country. Indeed, Obama's strategy in Iraq will likely be defined by "no risks," so that if Iraq founders, the blame will be laid on the previous administration.

Winning in Afghanistan

The situation in Afghanistan is different. There, Obama will need to make some immediate decisions his first weeks or even days in office. We are involved in a counterinsurgency

Robert D. Kaplan, "Obama's Afghanistan Hurdles," *The Atlantic*, December 12, 2008. Reproduced by permission of the author.

that it appears we are losing. The Taliban [a fundamentalist Islamic militia] has a credible presence in most parts of the country and the additional troops we deploy there may have to go to Kabul [Afghanistan's capital] to defend the capital itself from enemy attack. That's how bad the situation is.

[President Barack Obama should] make it known . . . that one of his highest priorities is getting [military] trainers to Afghanistan.

Beyond the immediate threat to Kabul, we need to start winning the counterinsurgency. The way to neutralize insurgents is not by fighting them directly but by getting well-trained and motivated indigenous forces to do the fighting for you. That way you win the support of the people, because the population cannot be expected to fight on the side of foreigners. In short, we can only eventually win in Afghanistan by growing the Afghan National Army. Afghanistan has a population of 32 million compared with Iraq's 27.5 million. It is also a more sprawling country, riven by mountains to a much greater extent than the flat Mesopotamian heartland. Yet the Afghan army, at 70,000 men, is considerably less than a third the size of Iraq's. We've shown in Iraq that we know how to grow armies. The challenge Obama faces is providing us with the wherewithal to do just that.

Army Maj. Gen. Robert W. Cone, who leads the Combined Security Transition Command-Afghanistan, has said that he needs 3,300 more military advisors to help train the Afghan army. Those advisors must come from the ranks of the U.S. Army. They should come from operational units that have actually served in the field in Afghanistan or Iraq. You want only the very best doing the training and motivation of new Afghan recruits. So one would think that Army headquarters at the Pentagon would be rushing the best trainers out to Afghanistan. But that isn't happening as quickly as it might, according to some. Here is where Obama can be helpful. He can make it known ... that one of his highest priorities is getting trainers to Afghanistan. That will give the Army the incentive it needs to expedite this process.

Financing the Afghan Army

But there is a larger question: who will finance this enlarged Afghan army that really should grow to roughly the size of Iraq's? Given that: 1) Afghanistan is a war supported by our NATO [North Atlantic Treaty Organization, an alliance of European and North American countries] allies; 2) that countries like India, Saudi Arabia, and Russia all have a stake in a non-radical and stable Afghanistan; and 3) that U.S. forces have done the lion's share of the fighting, these countries should be willing to pay for this benefit.

But it is unclear that they are. Here is where Obama needs to enter the fray early on. He is going to have enormous political capital his first months in office. During the U.S. election I was in India, which is a place where, because of the dramatic development in bilateral relations under his administration, President George W. Bush is not unpopular. But Obama's election electrified India with hope. Not only is Obama's transformative power abroad not to be exaggerated, but he will probably add to his political capital initially with symbolic gestures like—as has been reported likely—closing Guantanomo Bay and giving a major speech to the Islamic world in a Moslem capital. Obama needs to start spending this capital. And he should start by pressuring allies to help out more in Afghanistan, with more troops and more money.

In short, Obama needs to boil Afghanistan down to a number of factors where his pressure and influence can directly and dramatically help, and then apply himself immediately. Jump-starting Afghanistan and nurturing Iraq in its year of elections in 2009 should hopefully give him the space he needs to bear down on the problems of the U.S. economy.

Peace Must Be Made with the Taliban

Mustafa Qadri

Mustafa Qadri is the Middle East and South Asia Correspondent for NewMatilda.com, *an independent Australian Web site of news, analysis, and satire.*

"You are with us, or you are with the terrorists," declaimed [former] President George [W.] Bush in his now infamous speech to Congress following the September 11, 2001 attacks on the United States.

Now, the US is thinking of talking to the terrorists. . . .

Changing U.S. Policy

[In October 2008] the *Wall Street Journal* reported on a "policy review" in which the Bush Administration [was] considering opening talks with elements of the Taliban [a fundamentalist Islamic militia] in Afghanistan. In neighbouring Pakistan, the US has endorsed a Pakistan Government initiative to arm tribal militias, or lashkars, to hunt or recruit pro-Taliban militants in that country.

"Ultimately," says US Secretary of Defence Robert Gates, "there has to be . . . reconciliation [with the Taliban] as part of a political outcome to this."

[U.S. General David Petraeus] supports talks with what he calls "reconcilable elements" within the Taliban.

It is difficult to calculate the internal dynamics within the Bush Administration that . . . led to this dramatic policy shift.

Mustafa Qadri, "Is It Time to Make Peace with the Taliban?" *NewMatilda.com*, October 31, 2008. Reproduced by permission.

The US has come a long way since the day, in February 2002, that then-Taliban Foreign Minister Maulvi Wakil Ahmad Mutawakkil approached US officials to initiate a dialogue. Mutawakkil was arrested and spent the next four years at Guantanamo Bay [U.S. detention facility in Cuba]. The world's superpower may now be rueing the missed opportunity.

There have been suggestions that General David Petraeus—former commander of US forces in Iraq and [now] commander of all US forces in East Africa, the Middle East and Central Asia—has been spearheading the push for a more conciliatory approach to the Taliban. He supports talks with what he calls "reconcilable elements" within the Taliban.

Petraeus' endorsement stems from the success of a similar reconciliation effort, known as the Sunni Awakening, launched in Iraq when he was in charge of US forces there. Under the Sunni Awakening, thousands of Sunni militants, many of whom fought the US when it invaded the country in 2003, were paid by the US to fight Al Qaeda [an international terrorist network led by Osama bin Laden] and their allies.

Of course paying tribal militants to fight for Western forces is not a novel solution to Afghanistan's problems. It is a tactic used from the onset of the US invasion of the country in October 2001. It was also used during the Soviet occupation from 1978 to 1989 and, intermittently, by the British, a century earlier. Sadly, the tactic has made Afghanistan more volatile, not less.

The Americans are not the only ones now openly speaking of dialogue with the Taliban.

Yet it is clear that the US is becoming increasingly desperate for a policy shift towards the Taliban in Afghanistan....

[President] Barack Obama ha[s] publicly stated that [he] . . . will escalate the US military presence in Afghanistan. Obama, [has stated] . . . that his Administration would even consider unilateral attacks in Pakistan in the pursuit of Al Qaeda militants. That may not seem the strongest evidence for negotiations with the Taliban, but future strikes may target only those pro-Taliban militants that refuse overtures from the US.

Other Diplomatic Overtures to the Taliban

The Americans are not the only ones now openly speaking of dialogue with the Taliban.

Britain's top soldier and diplomat in Afghanistan, the UN's [United Nations] special envoy and the Chief of the French Army have all already concluded that peace in Afghanistan can only be secured through dialogue with the Taliban.

These comments represent an astonishing reversal of political calculations in Afghanistan. Last year [2007] President Hamid Karzai expelled two European diplomats for seeking to negotiate a truce with the Taliban in Helmand province.

In contrast, this year pro-Taliban militants and the Afghan Government have held several meetings with a view to the former swapping weapons for political representation.

In September [2008], during the Muslim holy month of Ramadan, the Saudi Government hosted a week of talks between the Afghan Government and elements of the Taliban and aligned militias. Although largely an ice breaker, the talks, which involved the Afghan President's brother, Qayyum Karzai, reflect the political vacuum created by the US occupation of the country since October 2001. While Western governments still mull over the prospect, Kabul and Riyadh [the capital of Saudi Arabia] have been quick to pitch a political settlement to the Taliban and other disaffected, predominantly Pashtun [a large Afghan tribe], tribes that have aligned themselves with the jihadi [holy war] movement.

According to the *Washington Post*, Afghan Taliban leader Mullah Omar said he would consider ending ties with Al

Qaeda, following a demand voiced by the Karzai Administration during the Saudi peace talks. The veracity of this claim remains to be determined.

Another initiative known as the "Mini-Jirga" (or tribal meeting) has seen Afghan and Pakistan Government officials and tribal chiefs meet to discuss ways to develop dialogue and reconciliation with the Taliban and other warring militants.

Both Governments agreed to hold talks with militants if they abided by the Afghan and Pakistan constitutions, a move calculated to compel the Taliban to accept a political solution. Significantly, however, Pakistan and Afghanistan backed down on an original demand that the militants first renounce violence.

In response, a Taliban spokesperson was quoted as saying that the movement would not support the Jirga's proposals until all foreign troops had left Afghanistan. Another told *Al Jazeera* [an Arabic news channel] that the Taliban would not accept portfolios within the Karzai Government either.

That has been a consistent demand from the jihadi movement, a demand that has been backed by a string of attacks in the country, some of which have targeted foreign aid workers.

Such violent intransigence may suggest that a negotiated settlement of hostilities is unlikely to materialise any time soon.

Alternatively, it may mean that the Islamic movement once famed for its rigid doctrines and strict fealty [fidelity] is splintering into different camps with varying degrees of antipathy towards the Western presence in Afghanistan or the Government it props up. If that is the case, negotiations will prove to be an equivocal solution.

A Regional Solution to Terrorism Is Needed

Hamid Karzai

Hamid Karzai is the president of Afghanistan.

We began a journey in Afghanistan seven years ago with the war that ousted the Taliban from power. Much has been accomplished along the way, for Afghanistan and for the world.

In less than 45 days in 2001, we Afghans were freed from the menace of terrorism and the Taliban. Back then, Afghanistan's people held great hopes for an immediately wonderful future. Some of those hopes were fulfilled. Our children are back in school. Roughly 85% of Afghans now have access to some health care, up from 9% before 2001. Child mortality—among the worst in the world in 2001—has dropped by 25%. Democracy, a free press, economic gains, and better livelihoods—all of that is there.

But, sadly, we are still fighting the Taliban and al-Qaida. What have we not done right that makes us—and the rest of the world—less secure?

After the liberation in 2001, the international community concentrated on Afghanistan alone as the place to tackle extremism and terrorism, while we Afghans argued that our country is not the right place to fight. The war on terror cannot be fought in Afghan villages. Instead, a regional approach was and is needed. It must be concentrated on the sanctuaries of those who train, equip, and motivate the extremists and send them out to hurt us all.

But we were not heard, and regardless of whether that was the result of a lack of knowledge or a lack of will, events have proven us right. Unfortunately, for the past two years, Pakistan has been affected as much or perhaps more than Afghanistan. Almost the entire tribal belt along the Pakistan/Afghanistan border is suffering.

> *The war on terror cannot be fought in Afghan villages. Instead, a regional approach . . . is needed.*

Just as schools were burned in Afghanistan from 2004 onwards, for the past year schools in Pakistan—especially for girls—have been reduced to ashes, leaving 80,000 children without facilities. Bridges have been blown up, soldiers and police killed; bombs have exploded from Karachi to Lahore to Islamabad. The violence has spread to India as well, with bombings in Gujarat, Bangalore and Delhi.

So the problem is regional, and it concerns institutional support for extremism that incites terrorism. Unless we collectively address the roots of the problem by ending that support, as well as financial support for radicalism in all forms, we will not defeat terrorism.

This has not been properly understood in the West, which has been fighting the symptoms of terrorism, but has failed to attack its underlying causes. Fortunately, today I see signs of recognition of this malaise. And democratic change in Pakistan is good news for Afghans, Pakistani people, and, by extension, many others around the world.

Pakistan's new president, Asif Ali Zardari, has suffered from terrorism as we have suffered. His wife, Benazir Bhutto, was murdered by terrorists. I visited Pakistan for President Zardari's inauguration, and for the first time I saw a dim ray of hope. If we can all work together—Afghanistan, Pakistan, India, the United States, and our allies—I see a possibility of moving beyond the days when a government thinks it needs extremism as an instrument of policy. When all governments in the region reject extremism, there will be no place for extremists, and terrorism will wither away.

But this also requires helping those people who, out of desperation, have fallen prey to extremist forces. Last year, I pardoned a 14-year-old boy from the Pakistan tribal area in Waziristan who had come to Afghanistan to blow himself up in a suicide bombing. Only utter hopelessness can drive so young a man to such an act. We must rescue these people by giving them a better future, which only more education and new opportunities can bring.

Desperation and poverty are the tools used by evil forces to raise their terrorist cadres. But that environment will not change if political will is lacking, and if there is no action by the US and the governments of the region to get our economies to create jobs that offer hope.

When all governments in the region reject extremism, there will be no place for extremists, and terrorism will wither away.

Moreover, in order to deny terrorists institutional support, we must bring institutional strength to Afghanistan. We must enable Afghans to look after themselves and defend their country, to have a future, to have hope of raising their children.

Recently, I spoke to an Afghan man very close to me. He has a son who works in the Afghan Foreign Office. That young man was born in the US but returned to Afghanistan four years ago. The father asked, "Do you think I should take my son back to the US?" I said, "Why? Let him live here, let him work here, let him be an Afghan." He said, "Yes, but will he have a future?"

A viable future means security as well as bread. We have started to bring hope by educating young Afghans, but we have not yet succeeded in bringing them a secure life, free from the danger of bombs and aerial bombardment. Only when that happens will the country be secure. And if the two other conditions are fulfilled—removal of political backing for radicalism and help for the desperate—we will have a safer life not only in Afghanistan, but in Pakistan, India, and the rest of the world.

Organizations to Contact

The editors have compiled the following list of organizations concerned with the issues debated in this book. The descriptions are derived from materials provided by the organizations. All have publications or information available for interested readers. The list was compiled on the date of publication of the present volume; the information provided here may change. Be aware that many organizations take several weeks or longer to respond to inquiries, so allow as much time as possible.

Afghan Relief Organization (ARO)
PO Box 866, Cypress, CA   90630
(877) 276-2440
Web site: www.afghanrelief.org

The Afghan Relief Organization is a humanitarian organization established in 1997 in response to the economic and physical hardships suffered by the Afghan people after decades of war. It is a volunteer organization funded by public donations that provides relief supplies and it runs several health, literacy, and other programs to help the poor in Afghanistan. The ARO Web site contains an overview of Afghanistan, materials teachers can use to educate students about Afghanistan, and links to newsletters discussing ARO news and activities.

Afghanistan Red Crescent Society
PO Box 3066, Kabul, Afghanistan
0093 79 385 533 • fax: 00932 290 097
e-mail: fatigli@yahoo.com
Web site: www.ifrc.org/address/af.asp

The International Federation of Red Cross and Red Crescent Societies is the world's largest humanitarian organization, providing relief assistance around the world. The Red Crescent is used in place of the Red Cross in many Islamic countries. The group's mission is to improve the lives of vulnerable people, especially those who are victims of natural disasters, poverty, wars, and health emergencies. A search of the organization's Web site produces numerous documents relevant to Afghanistan. The Web site also contains a section on "Where We Work," which provides specific information about the group's activities in Afghanistan.

Human Rights Watch (HRW)

350 Fifth Ave., 34th Fl., New York, NY   10118-3299
(212) 290-4700
e-mail: hrwnyc@hrw.org
Web site: www.hrw.org

Human Rights Watch is an independent organization dedicated to defending and protecting human rights around the world. It seeks to focus international attention on places where human rights are violated, give voice to the oppressed, and hold oppressors accountable for their crimes. A search of the HRW Web site produces numerous reports on human rights in Afghanistan, including "Afghanistan: Return of the Warlords" and "Afghanistan: US Investigation of Airstrike Deaths 'Deeply Flawed.'"

Institute for Afghan Studies (IAS)

e-mail: info@institute-for-afghan-studies.org
Web site: www.institute-for-afghan-studies.org/

Funded and run by young Afghan scholars from around the world, the Institute for Afghan Studies seeks to promote a better understanding of Afghanistan through scholarly research and studies. The IAS Web site provides a wealth of information on the history and politics of Afghanistan, including weekly political analyses, reports, articles, and biographical information about key figures in Afghanistan's politics. Examples of publications include "One Scary Voter Registration at a Time" and "Afghan Economy in the War and Pre-War Period."

Islamic Republic of Afghanistan/Office of the President
93 (0) 797 163 355
e-mail: spokesperson@afghanistangov.org
Web site: www.president.gov.af/english/contact_the_spokes
person.mspx

This central Web site of the Afghanistan government provides information on Afghanistan's president, National Assembly, constitution, cabinet, departments, and commissions. It contains news reports, presidential speeches and decrees, press releases and statements, as well as links to other government-affiliated Web sites.

NATO in Afghanistan
Blvd. Leopold III, Brussels, Belgium   1110
e-mail: natodoc@hq.nato.int
Web site: www.nato.int/issues/afghanistan/index.html

NATO in Afghanistan is part of the official Web site for the North Atlantic Treaty Organization (NATO), an alliance of 28 countries from Europe and North America committed to fulfilling the joint security goals of the 1949 North Atlantic Treaty. The Afghanistan section of the Web site provides an overview of NATO's interests and mission in Afghanistan and includes a link to the International Security Assistance Force (ISAF), a NATO military force that provides support to the Afghan government to help with security, reconstruction, and development.

Revolutionary Association of the Women of Afghanistan (RAWA)
PO Box 374, Quetta, Pakistan
0092-300-5541258 • fax: 0044-870-8312326 (UK)
e-mail: rawa@rawa.org
Web site: www.rawa.org/

The Revolutionary Association of the Women of Afghanistan was established in Kabul, Afghanistan, in 1977 as an independent political/social organization of Afghan women fighting for peace, freedom, and democracy in Afghanistan. The founders were Afghan women intellectuals, and RAWA's objective was to involve Afghan women in acquiring women's human rights and establishing an Afghan government based on democratic and secular values. RAWA also solicits public donations for relief aid and projects to help schools, orphanages, and women's cooperatives. RAWA's Web site includes press statements and speeches, as well as links to news, reports, and articles on political, social, and economic issues in Afghanistan. Recent publications include "An Overview on the Situation of Afghan Women" and "Some of the Restrictions Imposed by Taliban on Women."

United Nations Development Programme (UNDP)
1 United Nations Plaza, New York, NY   10017
(212) 906-5315 • fax: (212) 906-5001
e-mail: HZ@undp.org
Web site: www.undp.org

The United Nations Development Programme is an organization created by the United Nations to promote global development and help connect developing countries to knowledge, experience, and resources to help their people build a better life. Among other activities, the UNDP coordinates the efforts to reach the Millennium Development Goals, a commitment by world leaders to cut world poverty in half by 2015. A search of the UNDP Web site leads researchers to information about UNDP efforts in Afghanistan, including efforts to reduce poverty, promote democratic governance, and foster security.

U.S.-Afghan Women's Council
(202) 312-9664 • fax: (202) 312-9663
Web site: http://usawc.state.gov

The U.S.-Afghan Women's Council, a project of the U.S. State Department, was created on January 28, 2002, with a joint announcement from U.S. President George W. Bush and Afghanistan President Hamid Karzai. Its purpose is to promote private/public partnerships between U.S. and Afghan institutions and mobilize private resources to help Afghan women to gain skills and education and to play a role in the reconstruction of Afghanistan. The Web site includes information on council projects, as well as news, speeches, fact sheets, and press releases about issues affecting Afghan women.

U.S. Department of State
2201 C St. NW, Washington, DC   20520
(202) 647-4000
Web site: www.state.gov

The Department of State is a federal agency that advises the president on issues of foreign policy. Its Web site includes a "countries" section that provides a great deal of information about the country of Afghanistan, including an overview of the nation and materials relating to reconstruction, U.S. aid, and NATO's involvement in the country.

Bibliography

Books

Sarah Chayes   *The Punishment of Virtue: Inside Afghanistan After the Taliban.* New York: Penguin Press HC, 2006.

Anthony H. Cordesman   *The Lessons of Afghanistan: War Fighting, Intelligence, and Force Transformation.* Washington, DC: Center for Strategic & International Studies, 2002.

Robert D. Crews and Amin Tarzi, eds.   *The Taliban and the Crisis of Afghanistan.* Boston: Harvard University Press, 2008.

Dexter Filkins   *The Forever War.* New York: Knopf, 2008.

James W. Fiscus   *America's War in Afghanistan.* New York: Rosen Publishing Group, 2004.

Norman Friedman   *Terrorism, Afghanistan, and America's New Way of War.* Annapolis, MD: U.S. Naval Institute Press, 2003.

Gianni Giacomelli   *The Face of Afghanistan—Portraits and Life of a Wounded Land.* www.Lulu.com, 2007.

Musa Khan Jalalzai   *The Pipeline War in Afghanistan: Oil, Gas and the New Energy Great Game in Central Asia.* Pakistan: Sang-e-Meel Publications, 2003.

Seth G. Jones   *In the Graveyard of Empires: America's War in Afghanistan.* New York: W.W. Norton & Co., 2009.

Kenneth Katzman   *Afghanistan: Post-war Governance, Security, and U.S. Policy.* Hauppauge, NY: Nova Science Publishers, 2008.

Jagmohan Mehar   *America's Afghanistan War: The Success That Failed.* India: Kalpaz Publications, 2004.

Ursula Meissner   *Afghanistan: Hope and Beauty in a War-torn Land.* Germany: Bucher-Lounge, 2008.

Eric Micheletti   *SPECIAL FORCES: War Against Terrorism in Afghanistan.* France: Histoire and Collections, 2003.

Matthew J. Morgan   *A Democracy Is Born: An Insider's Account of the Battle Against Terrorism in Afghanistan.* Westport, CT: Praeger Security International, 2007.

Ahmed Rashid   *Descent into Chaos: The United States and the Failure of Nation Building in Pakistan, Afghanistan, and Central Asia.* New York: Viking Adult, 2008.

Paul Rogers   *A War on Terror: Afghanistan and After.* London: Pluto Press, 2004.

Periodicals

Jon Lee Anderson   "The Taliban's Opium War: The Difficulties and Dangers of the Eradication Program," *The New Yorker*, July 1, 2009. www.newyorker.com/reporting/2007/07/09/070709fa_fact_anderson.

Aryn Baker   "Facing Reality in Afghanistan: Talking with the Taliban," *TIME*, Oct. 13, 2008. www.time.com/time/world/article/0,8599,1849456,00.html.

BBC Persian   "Human Rights Violation in Afghanistan 'Has Doubled:' 'Three Thousand Cases in Six Months,'" Oct. 2, 2008. Translated and reprinted at www.rawa.org/temp/runews/2008/10/02/human-rights-violation-in-afghanistan-and-8220-has-double dand-8221_9834.html.

Barry Bearak and David Rohde   "The Other War: Iraq Gets Most of the Headlines, But the War in Afghanistan May Prove to Be More Important in the Fight Against Terrorism," *New York Times Upfront*, Jan. 3, 2008. Reprinted at http://findarticles.com/p/articles/mi_m0BUE/is_/ai_n27476580.

Greg Bruno   "Influence Peddlers: Saudi Arabia May Be Making More Than Just Peace with the Taliban," *Newsweek*, Dec. 11, 2008. www.newsweek.com/id/173828?tid=relatedcl.

Robert Fulford "The Afghanistan War Is Just,"
National Post, Nov. 10, 2007.
www.nationalpost.com/scripts/
story.html?id=f20865e5-0e70-4
caa-8243-3fc224daf8c6&k=60790.

Sharif Ghalib "Afghanistan: 2009 Presidential
Election a Litmus Test for
Legitimacy," *Afghan Online Press*, Jan.
9, 2009. www.aopnews.com/opinion/
ghalib_elections.shtml.

Terry Glavin "Young Afghan Democracy Facing Its
First Major Test: Country Nervously
Prepares for '09 Elections," *Vancouver
Sun*, Nov. 13, 2008.
www.canada.com/vancouversun/news/
story.html?id=fd31d1a3-a59d-4e1b-b9
e4-233466268f16.

Anand Gopal "Who Are the Taliban?" *The Nation*,
Dec. 3, 2008. www.thenation.com/
doc/20081222/gopal?rel=rightside
accordian.

Jon Hemming "Taliban in 72 Pct of Afghanistan,
Think-Tank Says," *Reuters*, Dec. 8,
2008. www.reuters.com/article/
homepageCrisis/idUSISL26617._
CH_.2400.

Jacob G. "The War on Afghanistan Was
Hornberger Wrong, Too," *The Future of Freedom
Foundation*, Oct. 19, 2007.
www.fff.org/freedom/fd0707a.asp.

Joe Klein   "The Aimless War: Why Are We in
                         Afghanistan?" *TIME*, Dec. 11, 2008.
                         www.time.com/time/world/article/
                         0,8599,1865730,00.html.

Mark Mazzetti   "U.S. Study Is Said to Warn of Crisis
and Eric Schmitt   in Afghanistan," *New York Times*, Oct.
                         8, 2008. www.nytimes.com/
                         2008/10/09/world/asia/09afghan.
                         html?_r=3&hp&oref=slogin&oref=
                         slogin&oref=slogin.

Ron Moreau and   "Dam Busters: Coalition Attacks
Sami Yousafzai   Have Forced the Taliban to Change
                         Its Tactics in Afghanistan. Leaders of
                         the Fundamentalist Movement Say
                         It's Going to Get More Deadly,"
                         Newsweek, Apr. 18, 2008.
                         www.newsweek.com/id/132684.

Caryle Murphy   "Jihadis Shift Attention to War in
                         Afghanistan: Afghan and NATO
                         Officials Are Seeing a Rise in
                         Numbers of Foreign Fighters in
                         Afghanistan at the Same Time US
                         Officials Say Attacks by Al Qaeda in
                         Iraq Have Sharply Dropped,"
                         Christian Science Monitor, Aug. 18,
                         2008. www.csmonitor.com/
                         2008/0819/p01s02-wome.html.

New York Times   "The Good War: Still to Be Won,"
                         Aug. 20, 2007. www.nytimes.com/
                         2007/08/20/opinion/20mon1.html?
                         _r=1&hp&oref=slogin.

Pam O'Toole   "No 'Real Change' for Afghan
                       Women: Women Reporting Rape
                       Run the Risk of Being Imprisoned
                       for Having Sexual Intercourse
                       Outside Marriage," *BBC News*, Oct.
                       31, 2006. Reprinted at
                       www.rawa.org/womankind.htm.

David Rohde and   "How a 'Good War' in Afghanistan
David E. Sanger   Went Bad," *New York Times*, Aug. 12,
                       2007. www.nytimes.com/2007/
                       08/12/world/asia/12afghan.html?_r=2.

Sayed Salahuddin   "Afghanistan's Presidential Poll Set
                       for Late 2009," *Reuters North
                       American News Service*, Apr. 9, 2008.
                       www.reuters.com/article/worldNews/
                       idUSISL31462620080409.

Mark Sappenfield   "Rise in Crime, Kidnapping, Top
and Anand Gopal   Afghans' Worries," *Christian Science
                       Monitor*, Nov. 25, 2008.
                       www.csmonitor.com/2008/1125/
                       p05s01-wosc.html.

Liliana Segura   "Should Americans Really Consider
                       Afghanistan the 'Right' War?"
                       AlterNet, July 31, 2008.
                       www.alternet.org/blogs/waroniraq/
                       93455/should_americans_really_consider_
                       afghanistan_the_%22right%22_war/.

Lally Weymouth   "'A Surge Is Good:' Afghan President
                       Hamid Karzai Supports More U.S.
                       Troops in Afghanistan, But Also
                       Pushes for Training for His Forces,"
                       Newsweek, Sept. 27, 2008.
                       www.newsweek.com/id/161205.

Index